TRAILBLAZERS

TRAILBLAZERS

The Men and Women Who Forged the West

CONSTANCE JONES

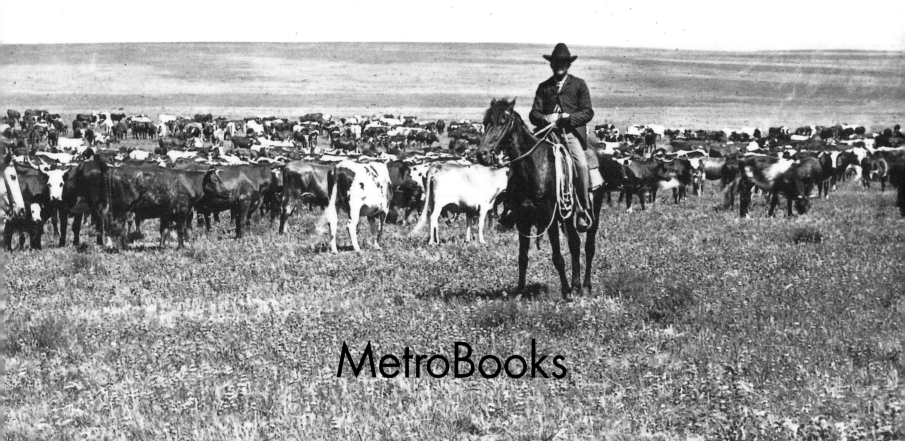

MetroBooks

MetroBooks

An Imprint of Friedman/Fairfax Publishers

© 1995 by Michael Friedman Publishing Group, Inc.

Library of Congress Cataloging-in-Publication Data available upon request

Editor: Benjamin Boyington
Art Director: Jeff Batzli
Designer: Kevin Ullrich
Photography Editor: Emilya Naymark

Color separations by Ocean Graphics International Company Ltd.
Printed in China by Leefung-Asco Printers Ltd.

For bulk purchases and special sales, please contact:
Friedman/Fairfax Publishers
Attention: Sales Department
15 West 26th Street
New York, NY 10010
212/685-6610 FAX 212/685-1307

DEDICATION

For my father, the history buff

ACKNOWLEDGMENTS

The author wishes to thank Ben Boyington for his editorial ministrations, Louise Quayle and Bree Burns for the loan of the valuable research materials, Sharyn Rosart for her developmental suggestions, and especially Heather Lewis for her perpetual support.

CONTENTS

CHAPTER 1

THE ORIGINAL PIONEERS

FOR EACH TRIBE OF MEN USEN CREATED HE ALSO MADE A HOME. IN THE LAND FOR ANY PARTICULAR TRIBE HE PLACED WHATEVER WOULD BE BEST FOR THE WELFARE OF THAT TRIBE. WHEN USEN CREATED THE APACHES, HE ALSO GAVE THEM THEIR HOMES IN THE WEST. HE GAVE THEM SUCH GRAINS, FRUITS, AND GAME AS THEY NEEDED TO EAT.... HE GAVE THEM A PLEASANT CLIMATE AND ALL THEY NEEDED FOR CLOTHING AND SHELTER WAS AT HAND. THUS IT WAS IN THE BEGINNING: THE APACHES AND THEIR HOMES EACH CREATED FOR THE OTHER BY USEN HIMSELF. WHEN THEY ARE TAKEN FROM THESE HOMES THEY SICKEN AND DIE.

—APACHE ORIGIN MYTH

The nineteenth century brought to the North American continent a mass migration known as the opening of the American West. White settlers crossed the land by wagon train and in cattle drives, on horseback and by railroad. These Americans and Europeans set out to tame the wilderness and make their fortunes. The lush forests, grassy plains, forbidding deserts, and foggy coastlands had sustained Native Americans for thousands of years, but white Americans and Europeans saw North America as an unclaimed territory free for the taking. In their optimism and innocence, they called the continent the New World, even though it had long been home to millions of people and hundreds of cultures.

In fact, North America had been settled much earlier. Migrant hunters from Asia came during the Ice Age—as long as thirty-five thousand years ago—when the frozen seas revealed a land bridge across the Bering Strait. Tracking mammoths, mastodons, and other game, the hunters wandered from Siberia to Alaska. As these first pioneers made their way south and east across North America, a wide variety of cultures emerged.

Long before white people arrived, several great civilizations had risen and fallen in the American West. Between 100 B.C. and A.D. 700, along the Ohio, Mississippi, and Illinois rivers, the people of the Hopewell culture built large burial mounds, which contained stunning basketry, jewelry, and pottery. In the eighth century, the Mississippian culture appeared farther south. Its people built temple mounds in large, fortified ceremonial centers and practiced intensive agriculture. At its peak in the 1500s, the Mississippian culture reached from Florida to Texas and from Kentucky to Louisiana.

In the Southwest, the Anasazi culture emerged in the first century A.D. Its people advanced agriculture, village life, and ceramics to high levels of sophistication before the Pueblo culture came to dominate the region around A.D. 700. The Pueblo peoples built large compounds of mud-walled dwellings—which now bear the name of their builders—and then abandoned them for unknown reasons around 1450. The Pueblo Indians then split into groups such as the Hopi and the Zuni, settling throughout the region.

When whites first began to encroach on Indian lands, many civilizations were thriving in the American West. Along the northwest coast alone, nearly fifty distinct groups

The ancient civilizations of North America produced remarkable art and architecture. Discovered at the Turner Mound group near Cincinnati, Ohio, this clay figurine (left) of a Hopewell woman dates from 300 B.C. to A.D. 500, while the Mesa Verde Pueblo (above) dates from A.D. 1100 to 1300.

lived between the Cascade Mountains and the Pacific Ocean, including the coastal Salish, Chinook, and Tillamook. Peoples such as the Cayuse, Nez Percé, Coeur d'Alene, and Flathead occupied the Columbia Plateau between the Cascades and the Rockies. Along the California coast were the Yurok, Pomo, Miwok, and others, while across the Sierra Nevada lived Great Basin groups like the Ute, Paiute, and Shoshone. In the Southwest, along with the Pueblo peoples, were such cultures as the Navajo, Apache, Yuma, and Havasupai. And ranging across the Great Plains were the groups who are perhaps best known today: the Comanche, Kiowa, Cheyenne, Sioux, and others.

DISTRIBUTION OF NATIVE AMERICAN GROUPS IN THE WEST

THE WILL TO SUSTAIN

While some Native Americans lived as nomadic hunters and gatherers, others settled in villages and farmed. Hunters relied on spears, bows and arrows, clubs, snares, nets, lures, hooks, and other tools to fell game and catch fish. Gatherers cut wild plants with stone blades and prepared grains with a variety of grinding and milling implements. Farmers used digging sticks, hoes, and rakes in their labors, growing such crops as corn, beans, squash, tomatoes, potatoes, and sunflowers.

An exception to the rule, the people of the Pacific Northwest Coast inhabited permanent towns but did not farm. They lived off the extraordinarily rich land, which provided all the wild game and edible plants they needed, as well as a seemingly inexhaustible supply of salmon, whales, and other creatures from the rivers and sea. Their eastern neighbors on the Columbia Plateau hunted in the region's densely forested mountains, fished in its numerous lakes and rivers, and for-

aged for roots and berries. But they occasionally had to migrate as they exhausted local resources.

Living an exceptionally simple life, more than a hundred California cultures benefited from the mild climate along the Pacific coast. These people were nomadic fishers, hunters, and gatherers for whom the acorn was the main staple of an ample diet. To the east, the Great Basin peoples had a much harder lot. Their home, which extended as far north as Idaho and as far south as Arizona, was extremely arid. As a result, small, widely scattered bands were always on the move, hunting for antelope, rabbits, rodents, reptiles, and fish. More often, depending on their hunting fortunes, they ate roots, seeds, berries, and insects.

In the Southwest, the Pueblo peoples and many of their neighbors cultivated their own food, especially corn. The Navajo did some farming, but survived mostly by hunting and harvesting wild edible fruits,

berries, and plants. Among those in the region who did not farm were the nomadic Apache, hunter-gatherers who roamed between the Great Plains and the Southwest, raiding settlements for food and supplies. Throughout the region, a scarcity of rainfall often threatened an otherwise comfortable way of life. One Papago legend tells of the end of a worrisome drought, in the words of a pilgrim watched over on his journey by the creator, his Protector:

> Thus I spoke, to him, my guardian [lit. "made father"].
> "What will happen? Most wretched lies the earth which you have made. The trees which you have planted, leafless stand. The birds you threw into the air, they perch and do not sing. The springs of water are gone dry. The beasts which run upon the earth, they make no sound."
>
> Thus I said. "What will befall the earth which you have made?"
>
> Then, thus spake he, my guardian, "Is this so difficult? You need but gather [together] and recite the ritual. Then, knowing all is well, go to your homes...."
>
> Then in the west a wind arose, well knowing whither it should blow. Up rose a mist and towered toward the sky, and others stood with it, their tendrils touching. Then they moved. Although the earth seemed very wide, clear to the edge of it did they go. Although the north seemed very far, clear to the edge of it did they go.
>
> Then to the east they went, and, looking back, they saw the earth lie beautifully moist and finished. Then out flew Blue Jay shaman; soft feathers he pulled out and let them fall. The earth was blue (with flowers). Then out flew Yellow Finch shaman; soft feathers he pulled out and let them fall, 'til the earth was yellow (with flowers).
>
> Thus was it fair, our year.

Spirituality pervaded Native American life, not only in moments of prayer on the plains (bottom left), but in everyday life in villages like this Mandan settlement (top left) depicted by the nineteenth-century American painter George Catlin.

Before white traders, soldiers, and settlers arrived on the high plains, untold millions of buffalo dominated the landscape (left). The hunting peoples of the region made use of every part of the buffalo, even drying its meat into jerky (below) to sustain them on the trail.

On the plains, the peoples of the well-watered eastern prairies farmed and hunted small game. Farther west, the climate was drier and hunting and gathering were more important. Some groups straddled the two zones, farming around prairie villages while sending bands of hunters out to the Great Plains in search of buffalo. The entirely nomadic peoples of the high plains depended almost solely on the buffalo for survival. Traveling on foot (they did not acquire horses until whites imported them from Europe), they followed the vast herds to seasonal feeding grounds. The plains hunters used spears and bows and arrows, and occasionally drove their prey off cliffs. They roasted the meat fresh or dried it into jerky for sustenance when buffalo was scarce.

THE SKILL TO CREATE

Native North Americans fashioned their clothing, jewelry, shelter, tools, and weapons with social and spiritual concerns in mind. Clothing and ornamentation reflected social rank, as could the size, decoration, or location of a shelter. Designs executed in woodwork, weaving, basketry, ceramics, shellwork, and featherwork often had religious significance.

Among the most creative and prolific Native American artisans were the people of the Pacific Northwest Coast. To repel the frequent rain, they built sturdy gabled roofs on their roomy wooden houses. Clothing and blankets of shredded cedar bark and animal fur kept them warm and dry, as did basket-woven rain hats. The arts flourished as the rains fell, and the people decorated their bodies by piercing their noses and marking their skin with tattoos. They also ranked among the world's great woodworkers, carving elaborate canoes up to 60 feet (18.3m) long, as well as helmets, shields, masks, house posts, and door poles. Eventually, whites named the unique carved posts "totem poles" and mistakenly assumed they were a feature of all Indian cultures.

The basketry and dugout canoes of the plateau peoples reflect some Pacific Northwest influence, but the demands of life east of the Cascades allowed less time for creative endeavors. The people spent more energy on survival, digging round, earthen-roofed dwellings into the hillsides each autumn and moving into domed pole-and-reed mat structures each spring.

The warm and sunny weather of California allowed the locals to wear minimal clothing. Requiring little shelter as they migrated, they sometimes built rough conical or domed structures of brush, bark, and earth. The bounty of their home gave them time to develop crafts, such as basketry of the highest quality, but their nomadic habits called for a minimum of material possessions. Equally simple but far more austere was the life of the Great Basin peoples. Dressed in little more than sandals, they constructed *wickiups*—brush huts or lean-tos—for shelter. Their constant struggle to feed themselves left little time or energy for elegant crafts or decorative arts.

The more settled life of many southwestern peoples allowed distinctive art forms to emerge; indeed, the people of the Southwest were the only indigenous North Americans to weave on looms. When they were not cooking food or helping to build additions to the pueblo huts, Hopi and Zuni women made baskets and pottery decorated with elaborate designs. The Navajo, who lived in villages of *hogans* (low,

The indigenous cultures of the Pacific Northwest created fine crafts decorated with distinctive motifs. Tightly woven, broad-brimmed straw hats (above right) served a practical purpose in the rainy climate, while carved door poles (right) had a spiritual function—they were used to portray the peoples' history and myths.

domed shelters constructed of logs and mud), made elegant jewelry and blankets, as well as clothing of animal skins and plant fibers. The roaming Apache paid more attention to their marauding. Their shelter consisted of temporary wickiups, which could be assembled quickly from local materials and abandoned in a hurry.

Unlike the settled prairie peoples, who lived in circular earth and mud lodges, the nomadic hunters of the Great Plains lived in portable *tipis*. Until they acquired horses, they used dogs to drag their possessions on travois, slings of buffalo hide supported by tipi poles. Other parts of the buffalo that they did not eat were put to other uses; from the bones and horns they made utensils, and from the hides they made

The skilled women of the southwestern pueblo cultures wove blankets (left) that bore unique designs developed by their people over centuries (right).

robes, tipi covers, clothing, and moccasins. For the Plains Indian, every object was imbued with spiritual significance, as one Oglala man reflected:

What do you see here, my friend? Just an ordinary old cooking pot, black with soot and full of dents. It is standing on the fire...and the water bubbles and moves the lid as the white steam rises to the ceiling. Inside the pot is boiling water, chunks of meat with bone and fat, plenty of potatoes.... The bubbling water comes from the rain cloud. It represents the sky. The fire comes from the sun, which warms us all—men, animals, trees. The meat stands for the four-legged creatures, our animal brothers, who gave of themselves so that we should live. The steam is living breath. It was water; now it goes up to the sky, becomes a

cloud again. These things are sacred. Looking at that pot full of good soup, I am thinking how, in this simple manner, Wakan Tanka takes care of me.... We try to understand not with the head but with the heart, and we need no more than a hint to give us the meaning.

SOCIETY

The structure of Native American societies ranged from very casual to rigidly hierarchical. People organized to hunt, farm, wage war, conduct rituals, dispense justice, and socialize. Indian communities also entertained themselves with many different toys, games, and sports, as well as with gambling.

The complex and stable cultures of the Pacific Northwest Coast centered around wealth and prestige. Their hierarchy included nobility at the pinnacle of society and slaves taken in warfare at the bottom. In addition to slaves, wealth might consist of practical and decorative items, as well as songs and heraldic crests. The avid pursuit of status gave rise to a ritual known as the *potlatch*. To earn distinction, the host of a potlatch would invite friends and rivals to watch him destroy or give away baskets, blankets, carved boxes, sheets of copper, and other valuables. The more wealth he disposed of, the more power he gained. This form of competition often became a display of dizzying excess.

On the plateau, each small, semipermanent settlement had its own leader and hierarchy. Largely independent, the bands traded with one another and occasionally allied for hunting or defense against outsiders. A similar system of small, independent groups also appeared in California, where bands followed traditional annual migration routes. Many California cultures had a basic legal system that allowed injured or offended parties to receive payment from those who wronged them.

Such advanced social institutions were impossible for the far-flung bands of the Great Basin. The groups of twenty to thirty-five people struggled simply to feed themselves; several bands would camp together in winter. Waging war or building complex societies were luxuries they could not afford.

In the Southwest, wandering peoples such as the Navajo lived in autonomous bands within well-defined territories. Occasionally, bands of the same clan gathered to hunt or to conduct religious rituals. Settled Pueblo life was more ordered. The long history of these peoples, as well

Rituals such as the Mandan O-Kee-Pa ceremony witnessed by painter George Catlin (above) united the members of Native American communities. In many cultures, entire bands or clans gathered to make important decisions together (left).

as the architecture of their dwellings, produced close-knit communities. Among the Hopi, the Zuni, and others, the needs of the group superseded the needs of the individual; conformity to social norms was valued. When Apache raiders attacked a pueblo, tight social organization allowed the residents to move quickly in defense of their home. The Pueblo sense of community is reflected in this Zuni prayer of blessing for a newborn child:

> *Now this is the day. Our child, into the daylight you will go standing. Preparing for your day, we have passed our days.*
> *When all your days were at an end, when eight days were past, our sun father went in to sit down at his sacred place. And our night fathers, having come out standing to their sacred place, passing a blessed night, we came to day. Now this day our fathers, dawn priests, have come out standing to their sacred place. Our sun father, having come out standing to his sacred place, our child, it is your day.*
> *This day, the flesh of the white corn, prayer meal, to our sun father this prayer meal we offer. May your road be fulfilled, in your thoughts (may we live). May we be the ones whom your thoughts will embrace. For this, on this day, to our sun father we offer prayer meal.*
> *To this end may you help us all to finish our roads.*

The society of the plains peoples was far looser than that of the Pueblos. For the large, semipermanent settlements of the interior plains—especially the walled towns of the north—trade in furs and other goods was an important component of the economy. Commerce and agriculture required some social cooperation, but farther west the nomadic ways of the Great Plains allowed for little formal government. Under its own leader and council, each band set up seasonal tipi villages, but no chief oversaw an entire tribe. Bands traded with and raided one another to secure booty or earn honor as warriors. The

Whites arriving in the American West were especially intrigued by the plains Indians. Top left: George Catlin painted Old Bear, a Mandan medicine man, in 1832. Bottom left: Charles M. Russell painted this Blackfoot brave in 1858.

Blackfeet, Comanche, and Kiowa were known as the fiercest warriors on the plains.

THE SPIRITUAL LIFE

You see I am alive
You see, I stand in good relation to the earth
You see, I stand in good relation to the gods
You see, I stand in good relation to all that is beautiful
You see, I stand in good relation to you
You see, I am alive, I am alive

—Plains Indian prayer

Indian religion recognized the connections between every being, event, and object in the universe. Deeply respectful of the earth and all its creatures, the native North Americans placed their faith in supernatural forces that linked people with all living things. They viewed humans as the equals, not the masters, of animals and plants. Often described as a mother, the earth was cherished and thanked for providing the means of survival. A hunter's or farmer's success was believed to depend on personal harmony with natural forces. Survival and prosperity flowed not from struggle and achievement but from a respectful relationship with nature.

Central to Indian religious life were music, dance, and storytelling. The magic of these art forms was called upon to contact the spirit world, ensure a good harvest, prepare for a hunt or war, and to celebrate significant events. Drums, flutes, rattles, and other instruments accompanied the singing and dancing, while gestures and acting illustrated tales and myths.

The indigenous people of the Northwest Coast had especially lovely art forms to match their complex religious life. Powerful shamans (Native American priests) and secret societies performed masked ritual dances and ceremonies in honor of the many spirit beings that populated their cosmos. The beings, such as those in this origin myth of the Puget Sound Indians, were responsible for creation and destruction, good and evil:

Photographers reached the American West just as its original societies were being destroyed. They arrived just in time to immortalize the last of the great Indian leaders.

Long, long ago, some people on the earth...became so very wicked that Dokibatl, the Changer, sent a flood upon the earth. All living things were destroyed except one woman and one dog.... From the woman and the dog were born the next race of people. They walked on four legs and lived in holes in the ground.... Having no fire and no clothing, they suffered from both the heat and the cold....

At last the Changer sent a Spirit Man over the mountains.... First he called the people together for a big potlatch, the first

Every Native American society, whether in the Pacific Northwest (above) or on the plains (below right), employed religious rituals to summon assistance from the spirit world for hunters, warriors, and farmers.

The most prominent element of spiritual life on the plateau was the annual Winter Spirit dance, for which many Native American groups came together to seek contact with their guardian spirits. These communal religious rituals were led by shamans. The religious life of California peoples was also richly filled with festivals, games, initiation rites, dances, songs, ceremonial societies, and superstitions. By contrast, the religious activities and traditions of the Great Basin peoples were minimal, for the daily battle to feed themselves claimed most of their attention.

In the Southwest, the spiritual life of the Pueblo peoples centered around the *kiva*, a round, underground ceremonial structure that only men were allowed to enter. Within this structure, a great deal of the community's religious activity took place in secret, the main goal being to ensure a good harvest. The Hopi and Zuni also performed long public rituals associated with the

potlatch of all the Indians.... To the young men, the Spirit Man gave bows, arrows, and spears, and he taught all the young men how to use them. To the old men, he gave canoes. He showed them how to make canoes from cedar trees, how to make fishing spears and nets, and how to fish from the canoes....

In a big house he placed all the diseases and evil deeds known to the world since then. Then he called a certain family to him and made them the guardians of the building.... One day, when her father and mother went away from the house, the daughter saw her chance to peek into the Spirit Man's house. She had long wanted to see what was behind that door. So she undid the fastenings and pushed back the door a little distance. Out rushed all the creatures of the house—all the diseases and evil deeds and sorrows that have been in the world ever since.

corn-growing cycle. Shamans donned costumes and masks to impersonate benevolent spirits known as *kachinas*. While recounting myths, they distributed kachina dolls to the people. Other southwestern peoples had less elaborate practices but similar spiritual aims. In their religious life, for instance, the Navajo sought to achieve harmony with the universe.

Although quite different in many ways, the spiritual traditions of the plains peoples had some similarities to those of the Pueblo Indians. All-male secret societies performed many religious functions, while large public rituals allowed all members of the group to participate. Each year, related Great Plains bands gathered for enormous festivals, at which dances and rituals were performed to honor the spirits. The men of these cultures sought divine guidance through dreams, fasting, vision quests, and self-torture.

Dreams and visions gave many indigenous peoples throughout the American West a chillingly accurate glimpse of the tragic future that awaited them. Black Elk, an Oglala who published his memoirs after the whites had conquered the West, recounted one of these prophecies:

There was once a Lakota [Sioux] holy man, called Drinks Water, who dreamed what was to be; and this was long before the coming of the Wasichus [white men]. He dreamed that the four-leggeds were going back into the earth and that a strange race had woven a spider's web all around the Lakotas. And he said: "When this happens, you shall live in square gray houses, in a barren land, and beside those square gray houses you shall starve."

Imagery from plains Indian culture lingered in the American imagination long after the plains peoples disappeared, perhaps because their warriors fought the last and bloodiest battles against the white conquerors of the West.

CHAPTER 2

THE EUROPEAN TRAILBLAZERS

A S NEWS OF CHRISTOPHER COLUMBUS'S 1492 VOYAGE ACROSS THE ATLANTIC OCEAN SPREAD THROUGH EUROPE, MANY AMBITIOUS EUROPEAN EXPLORERS, MISSIONARIES, SOLDIERS, AND TRADERS RUSHED TO NORTH AMERICA. THE FIRST TO ESTABLISH A PRESENCE IN WHAT WOULD BECOME THE AMERICAN WEST WERE THE SPANISH, WHO PUSHED THEIR WAY NORTH FROM MEXICO AND THE CARIBBEAN.

Arriving from eastern Canada, the French spread across the continent's interior by following its rivers. The English, meanwhile, kept largely to the eastern seaboard, although a number of explorers and traders made sea voyages to the west coast. Eventually, Russians gained a foothold on the Pacific Northwest Coast. Before the colonies won their independence from England, white settlement in the American West was sparse and scattered. Nonetheless, European adventurers had an enormous impact on the indigenous peoples. Horses, guns, and whiskey forever changed Indian culture and played a central role in the white conquest of North America. The early arrivals of white people eased the way for later pioneers by acquainting Native Americans with European customs, and especially by whetting their appetite for European goods. The early white explorers also introduced diseases—smallpox, typhus, and cholera, among others—to which Native Americans had no immunity. Epidemics killed untold numbers of Indians, weakening their cultures and depopulating the land for the white settlers who would appear in the nineteenth century.

THE SPANISH

Spain dominated the American West throughout the 1500s, the first century of European enterprise in the New World. The Spanish *conquis-*

tadores came in search of gold and silver; equipped with firearms, armor, and horses, the invaders easily staked a claim to American soil. Finding little precious metal in the Southwest and California, they took what they could from the indigenous people and put them to work as slaves or serfs. At the same time, Spanish missionaries established mission stations throughout the Southwest and California and tried to convert the Indians to Catholicism.

The conquistadores' hunger for gold was sharpened by the success of Hernando Cortés, who made his conquest of Mexico from 1518 to 1522. Landing on the Gulf Coast near Veracruz with 555 soldiers and sixteen horses, he plundered the fabulous wealth of the Aztec Empire and sent it back to Spain. In 1532, Francisco Pizarro toppled the gold-rich Inca empire of Peru. The bounty found in Mexico and Peru fed rumors of other wealthy civilizations in the New World. These rumors evolved into the legend of El Dorado, a place said to be richer in gold than any country found before. Spurred by greed, conquistadores wandered far and wide. By the 1770s, New Spain reached north through Arizona and New Mexico to the San Francisco Bay, east along the Gulf of Mexico to Texas, and south to Guatemala. It also included much of what is now the southeastern United States.

The first Spaniards to enter the American West came there by accident. Led by the cruel and clumsy Panfilo de Narvaez, an expedition to Florida met defeat at the hands of the Apalachee Indians. The few Spanish survivors fled into the Gulf of Mexico on fragile, hastily constructed boats. The flimsy fleet was shipwrecked in the fall of 1528 on the coast of Texas; most of the men, including Narvaez, drowned. Among the eighty cast ashore, all but four eventually died. For six years, Alvar Núñez Cabeza de Vaca, a Moorish slave named Estevanico, and two other Spaniards lived with the Indians as virtual slaves. Cabeza de Vaca and Estevanico finally escaped and headed west, trekking across southern Texas, New Mexico, and Arizona. Along the way, the local people told them of Cibola, a golden, undiscovered land nearby. They reached Spanish territory in 1536. Estevanico tantalized the

From the sixteenth century to the American Revolution, thousands of ships sailed for the New World from Spain, France, England, Holland, Portugal, and other European nations.

The apparent success of Marcos inspired Spain's Mexican viceroy to commission another expedition. In 1540, Francisco Vásquez de Coronado headed north with an army of well-equipped horsemen and foot soldiers. He soon found out that Fray Marcos, who had come along as an adviser, was a liar. "We have all become very distrustful of the father provincial," he wrote, "and were dismayed to see that everything was the reverse of what he said."

As the Spaniards approached, the Pueblo peoples rejected Coronado's peaceful overtures. Near Hawikuh pueblo, several hundred Zuni warriors blocked the way. The conquistadores attacked and captured the pueblo within an hour, but Coronado was badly wounded. He sent Pedro de Tovar to subdue the Hopi pueblos, which was easily accomplished. According to Tovar, the Hopi "had heard that Cibola had been captured by very fierce people, who traveled on animals that ate people." Ordered by Coronado to look for a "great river" of which the Indians spoke, García López de Cárdenas came upon the Colorado River and the Grand Canyon, about which he reported:

> The men spent three days looking for a way down to the river; from the top it looked as if the water were a fathom across. But, according to the information supplied by the Indians, it must have been half a league wide. The descent was almost impossible.... From the top they could make out, apart from the canyon, some small boulders which seemed to be as high as a man. Those who went down and who reached them swore that they were taller than the great tower of Seville.

About this time, Coronado heard of Quivira, a gold-rich land to the northeast, where "everyone had their ordinary dishes made of wrought plate, and the jugs and bowls were of gold." Moving his headquarters to Tiguex, between present-day Albuquerque and Taos, New Mexico, he evicted the Indians from their pueblos there. When the people rebelled, Coronado destroyed the pueblos and had the Indians massacred or enslaved. The conquistador then set out for Quivira with the aid of some Indian guides. They took him on a wild-goose chase across the high plains of the Texas panhandle, where they found nothing but some bands of friendly but poor Apache. A member of that expedition noted that:

Spain's official justification for subjugating the indigenous peoples of the New World, among them the Incas of Peru, was to convert them from their "heathen" ways to Roman Catholicism.

Spanish residents of Mexico City with rumors of wealth to the north, but Cabeza de Vaca returned to Spain convinced that "these people [the Indians] are all very fond of romance, and are great liars."

Estevanico served as guide on an expedition led by a Franciscan monk, Fray Marcos de Niza, which left Mexico City for the north in 1539. Estavanico scouted ahead and sent dispatches back to Marcos, claiming he had found the seven great cities of Cibola. Estevanico was killed, however, when he threatened some Zuni, and Marcos returned to Mexico City, reporting that large, wealthy cities—as yet unseen—lay to the north.

these Indians subsist...entirely on cattle [buffalo], for they
neither plant nor harvest maize.... They are a gentle people,
not cruel, faithful in their friendship, and skilled in the use of
signs.... They have no permanent residence anywhere, since
they follow the cattle to obtain food.

Unimpressed by the Apache or the buffalo, Coronado finally learned the location of Quivira. Heading northeast to central Kansas, he found not a golden city but a cluster of Wichita villages. Disgusted, he killed his one remaining guide and returned to Mexico in 1542.

Conquistadores continued to roam the region looking for riches, in the process introducing the horse to the Indians of the Great Plains and the Great Basin. As horses spread across the land via trade, theft, and escape, the Indians adapted them for hunting and transportation. The horse increased the mobility of nomadic peoples and caused some settled village groups to "lose the corn" and become migratory hunters. Easier buffalo hunting increased tribal wealth and nourished Indian culture. A product of horse trading and wider travel, greater contact between Indian groups exposed them to new practices and ideas.

In only a few short years, the horse assumed a central place in Indian life across much of the American West. It became the subject of legends, poems, and songs:

Francisco Vásquez de Coronado and his men wandered the American Southwest for years in search of gold (above). Instead of El Dorado or the fabled city of Quivira, he found humble settlements and Indians who often resisted Spanish domination (left).

Its feet are made of mirage.

Its gait was a rainbow.

Its bridle of sun strings.

Its heart was made of red stone.

Its intestines were made of water of all kinds.

Its tail of black rain.

Its mane was a cloud with a little rain.

Distant lightning composed its ears.

A big spreading twinkling star formed its eye and
striped its face.

Its lower legs were white.

At night beads formed on its lips.

White shell formed its teeth.

A black flute was put in its mouth for a trumpet.

Its belly was made of dawn, one side white and one side
black.

—Navajo horse song

Believing the conquistadores to be gods, some Indians willingly offered what little gold they had and agreed to engage in Catholic conversion rituals (above left). The Spanish were able to build many missions (below) throughout the Southwest.

The Spanish made no effort to colonize the American West until 1598. That year, Juan de Oñate led a group of four hundred settlers north from Mexico and established his headquarters, called San Gabriel, at the San Juan pueblo north of Española on the Chama River. Dividing up the land, Oñate assigned friars to each district and established estates with Indian slaves for the Spanish settlers. In doing so, he destroyed a number of pueblos, killed hundreds of people, and took hundreds more captive. Scores of Indians fled to the mountains, where many starved or froze to death. Eventually, the chaotic colony failed, and Oñate returned to Mexico.

Pedro de Peralta had more success. Appointed governor of New Mexico in 1609, he founded the colony of Santa Fe with 250 Spanish colonists and seven hundred Mexican slaves. Other settlements soon appeared in New Mexico, peopled by Spaniards seeking their fortune. One such colonist was Fray Alonso de Benevides, who made this rather fanciful report to the king:

Above: The Spanish enslaved large numbers of Indians in the Southwest and treated them with great cruelty.

All this [land] is full of very great treasures of mines, very rich and prosperous in silver and gold; a thing which as a regular duty, as so devoted chaplains and vassals, we besought of God; and, making special effort by means of an intelligent person, we came to discover; for which, in the name of Your Majesty, we give Him infinite thanks.... I feel that if the [mines] were administered by persons of moderate greed, who would treat the Indians well and pay them for their work, conforming now at the beginning with their simple capacity, [which is] slack as to working, that...they themselves, seeing and knowing that they were not treated ill, and that they were paid for their work, would come to offer themselves for it. With this it would be easier for us ministers to reduce them to peace.

This advice was not heeded, however, and throughout the 1600s the Indians were treated very badly by the Spaniards and, rather than being "reduced to peace," they stubbornly practiced their now outlawed customs, beliefs, and rituals in secret. The friction sparked the Great Pueblo Revolt of 1680, spearheaded by a medicine man named Popé, in which Pueblo Indians throughout the colony burned churches and killed more than four hundred Spanish friars, soldiers, and colonists. Soon after, the Pueblo rebels joined with the Apache, took Santa Fe, and freed the Indian slaves; Pueblo country remained free for thirteen years. One vexed friar who visited the Southwest after the uprising wrote of the Indians, "They have been found to be so pleased with liberty of conscience and so attached to the worship of Satan that up to the present not a sign has been visible of their ever having been Christians."

The Spanish crushed the Pueblo rebellion by 1698, although they never reconquered the Hopi. Sparse colonial settlement slowly extended east into Texas and almost to the Mississippi River, and by 1740 the Spanish population of New Mexico had reached five thousand. To secure Spain's claim to California, a Spanish colonizing expedition traveled there in 1769. Fray Junipero Serra founded San Diego while Spanish soldiers and missionaries moved as far north as San Francisco Bay.

Serra established an extensive network of missions up and down the California coast, prompting a colleague to write later, "So incessant was the desire of our Venerable Father Junipero to found new missions that, dissatisfied with his efforts, he died with his thirst still unsatisfied." The California missions attracted groups of "mission Indians" who converted to Catholicism and came to depend on the missions for their livelihood. Even after Mexico won its independence from Spain in 1821 and took control of the Southwest and California, the Spanish missions remained an important feature of the American West.

THE FRENCH

Although small in numbers, French trappers, traders, missionaries, and explorers had a significant presence in the American West. They built up the highly profitable beaver-pelt trade and opened an enormous amount of territory to European influence. Traveling between far-flung trading posts and forts from the Great Lakes to New Orleans and from the Dakotas to the Southwest, this highly mobile population mingled with rather than displaced the indigenous peoples they encountered. Most were men who came without families in search of adventure. Among them were the fiercely independent *coureurs de bois* (runners of the woods) or *voyageurs*, who lived in the forests and adopted Indian survival techniques.

The few French subjects who had any desire to leave their homeland had more interest in turning a profit than in settling the wilderness. Because they did not attempt to conquer the Indians, take their land, or clear their hunting grounds, the French managed to remain on friendly terms with most indigenous groups for some time. Good Indian rela-

tions helped France to secure control of the waterways that gave them access to North America's interior.

French exploration and exploitation of the American West began late in the seventeenth century. In 1672 Louis de Buade, Comte de Frontenac et Palluau, became governor of New France (Canada) and sent Louis Joliet on an expedition to the Great Lakes. At the mission of Father Jacques Marquette, between lakes Michigan and Huron, Joliet convinced the Jesuit to join him. Together they followed the Illinois River to the Wisconsin River and the Wisconsin to the Mississippi. They traveled down the Mississippi as far as the Arkansas River, then turned back to avoid the Spaniards to the south. In honor of Louis XIV, they named the vast region Louisiana.

With the backing of Frontenac and King Louis, René-Robert Cavelier de La Salle set out to explore the interior of North America in 1682. Following the Mississippi all the way south (he was probably the first European to travel the length of this great river), he crossed Lake Ponchartrain and reached the Gulf of Mexico. On behalf of France, he laid claim to the entire area drained by the Mississippi, from the Great Lakes to the Gulf of Mexico and from the Appalachian Mountains to the Rocky Mountains. He returned to France in triumph.

Two years later, the king sent La Salle back to North America to build forts along the Mississippi. The explorer directed his ships across the Atlantic to the Caribbean, then across the Gulf of Mexico to find the river's mouth. Sailing too far west, the fleet landed at Matagora Bay in Texas. Despite all the evidence to the contrary, the delusional La Salle was convinced he had reached the Mississippi River Delta. Disease and Indian attacks started to kill off his men, but La Salle kept searching for the Mississippi. Becoming more and more deranged as time wore on, he continued his quest until 1687, when one of his men killed him.

French trappers learned new hunting and survival techniques from the Indians they met in the wilderness (above left). Benefiting from generally friendly Indian relations, French explorers such as La Salle, who reached Texas (left), ranged far afield.

Jean Baptiste le Moyne, Sieur d'Iberville, became governor of Louisiana and oversaw the region's exploration during the first half of the eighteenth century. Various French explorers charted the rivers of the continent's vast midsection, while traders built scattered fur-trading posts. Many of these adventurers never left the wilderness, preferring its simple rewards and challenges to the refined comforts and complications of "civilization." In his old age, one such coureur de bois recalled a life without worries, lived to the rhythm of songs sung while paddling canoes.

I have now been forty-two years in this country. For twenty-four I was a light canoe man.... No portage was too long for me; all portages were alike. My end of the canoe never touched the ground till I saw the end of [the portage].... Fifty songs a day were nothing to me, I could carry, paddle, walk and sing with any man I ever saw.... No water, no weather, ever stopped the paddle or the song. I have had twelve wives in the country; and was once possessed of fifty horses, and six running dogs, trimmed in the first style. I was then like a Bourgeois, rich and happy: no Bourgeois had better dressed wives than I; no Indian chief finer horses; no white man better harnessed or swifter dogs.... I wanted for nothing; and I spent all my earnings in the enjoyment of pleasure. Five hundred pounds, twice told, have passed through my hands; although I now have not a spare shirt to my back, nor a penny to buy one. Yet, were I young again, I should glory in commencing the same career again. I would spend another half-century in the same fields of enjoyment. There is no life so happy as a voyageur's life; none so independent; no place where a man enjoys so much variety and freedom as in the Indian country.

French relations with the Indians remained generally peaceful, but the arrival of these Europeans did serious harm to indigenous North

While French trappers in the interior often enjoyed peaceful solitude (left), traders who sailed to the Pacific Northwest and Alaska had to compete with other fortune hunters from many European nations (opposite, top).

American society. French authorities encouraged the Indians "to come and settle in common with the French, to live with them and raise their children according to our manners and customs." Many Native American women did marry Frenchmen, strengthening French-Indian ties but diluting Indian culture. Some French Catholic missionaries contributed to this dilution, working to wipe out native beliefs and traditions they did not understand. But even those who learned to respect Native American ways invariably spread European disease. The Indians sometimes blamed missionaries for the epidemics that followed their arrival, and a number of these missionaries were executed as a result.

Active trading with the French made many Indians dependent on European goods. As they competed fiercely for a share of the fur trade, many Indian groups abandoned their traditional respect for wildlife and ignored time-honored rituals of conservation. Those who traded with the French obtained whiskey and guns for the first time. Frequent and often violent drunkenness took a heavy toll on people who had never tasted alcohol before. Firearms improved their ability to defend themselves, but made intertribal warfare more deadly.

By the 1740s, French traders ranged as far west as Santa Fe, establishing a route from Missouri that would come to be known as the Santa Fe Trail. The Indians of the Southwest much preferred trading with the French to trading with the Spanish. The Spanish, they told the French, "bring us horses and a few knives and a few awls and a few axes...they are not like you, who give us great quantities of merchandise, such as we have never seen before." In an effort to protect their territory, the Spanish arrested many of the French traders and threw them into Mexican jails. But the inveterate wanderers continued to roam the continent, never quite settling down.

THE NORTHWEST

While the Spanish focused on the Southwest and the French occupied themselves with the interior, the English and the Russians turned their attention to the Pacific Northwest Coast. In 1577, Queen Elizabeth I of England commissioned Sir Francis Drake to challenge Spain in the New World. Drake sailed around South America and north to the coast of Oregon, which he reached in June 1579. Following the coastline, he cruised down to California and claimed it for England, ignoring Spain's prior claim. One of his men told of an encounter with California Indians:

> The people of the country, having their houses close by the waterside, showed themselves unto us, and sent a present to our General. When they came unto us, they greatly wondered at the things that we brought, but our General (according to his natural and accustomed humanity) courteously entreated them, and liberally bestowed on them necessary things to cover their nakedness, whereupon they supposed us to be gods.

Above: In 1741, Danish explorer Vitus Bering (left) contracted with Russia to chart the seas surrounding the Aleutian Islands (right), where he was shipwrecked. Below: Russian fur traders established many settlements and built numerous Russian Orthodox churches in Alaska.

In 1588, Drake led the British to victory over the Spanish Armada in the Caribbean, signaling the beginning of the end of Spanish dominance in North America. A century and a half later, Vitus Bering, a Dane working for Russia, sailed from Russia to Alaska across the Bering Strait. The Russians began an active trade in sea otter pelts with the indigenous Alaskans, and in 1783 founded the first permanent Russian settlement in the New World, on Kodiak Island. Moving down the coast, they set up trading posts as far south as northern California. Russian activity attracted other Europeans to the region's lucrative fur trade. English traders from Hudson's Bay pushed west into the Dakotas and down the Columbia River, and Captain James Cook sailed from England to the northwest coast. The Spanish sailed up the Pacific coast from California, as did the French.

Throughout the American West, the convergence of representatives of various European countries on lands desired by all led, not surprisingly, to war. Eighteenth-century North America was a battlefield on which European nations played out their rivalries. Most of the fighting took place in the East, but it made an indelible mark on the West. Spain took the side of France against England during the French and Indian War, which England won. Under the Treaty of Paris in 1763, France ceded Canada and all its land east of the Mississippi River to England and gave Louisiana west of the Mississippi (except New Orleans) to Spain as compensation for Spain's loss of Florida to England. Thus, when the thirteen British colonies won independence, the new United States took possession of all North American territory east of the Mississippi and south of the Great Lakes.

NORTH AMERICA, 1713

NORTH AMERICA, 1763

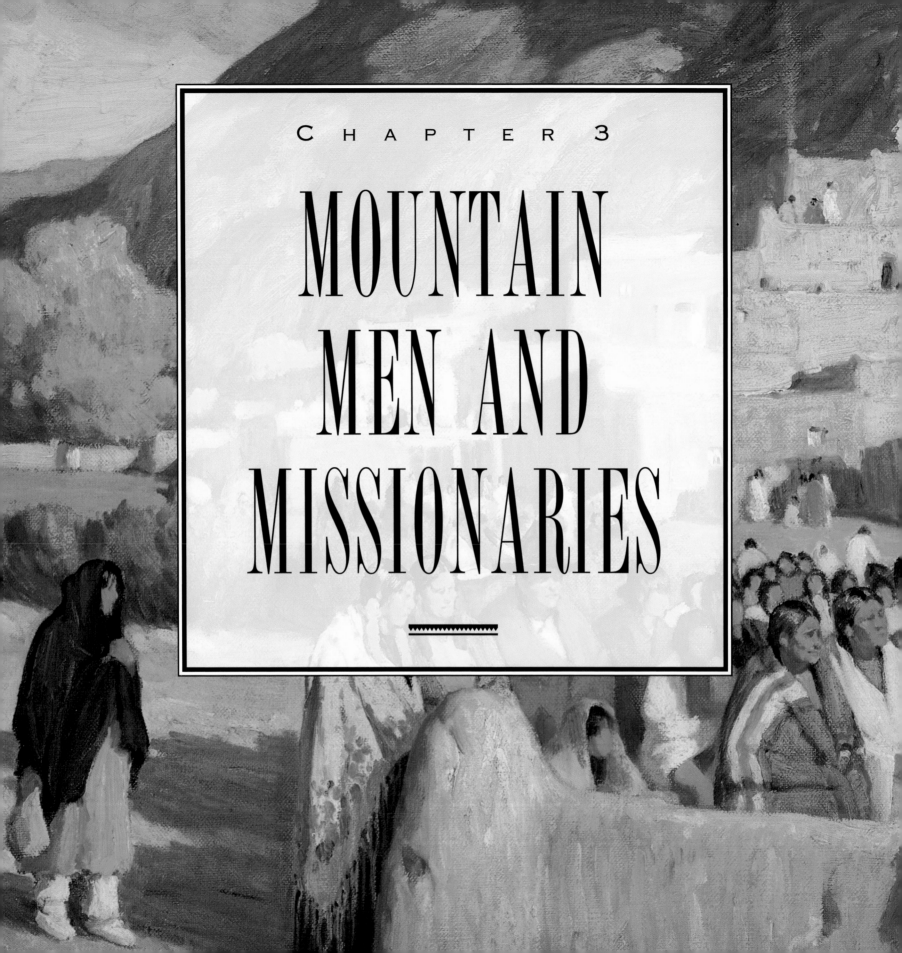

CHAPTER 3

MOUNTAIN MEN AND MISSIONARIES

At the end of the American Revolution, the United States was poised for expansion at least as far west as the Mississippi River. The nation's booming population clamored for more farmland, pushing farther into the continent's interior with each passing year. Leading the way into the unknown were a few hardy explorers and fur trappers who hoped to discover and exploit the untold resources of North America. The most determined of these intrepid souls ventured across the Mississippi River, out of U.S. territory, and into the American West. In 1792, Robert Gray and William Burroughs led an exploration of the Pacific Northwest Coast and the Columbia River. In 1794, on behalf of the Northwest Company, a Canadian fur-trading concern, an American named Andrew Henry followed the Madison River into the Rocky Mountains. And in 1802, James Purcell charted the Osage and Arkansas rivers on the Great Plains.

After winning its independence, the United States looked west toward its future. Lewis and Clark were in the vanguard of those who fulfilled John Quincy Adams's 1819 prophesy that the conquest of the West was "as much a law of nature...as that the Mississippi should flow into the sea."

Convinced of the West's potential, the U.S. government decided to buy the Louisiana territory from France, which had recently reacquired the enormous territory from Spain. Completed in 1804, the Louisiana Purchase more than doubled the land holdings of the United States, extending the country's boundaries to the Continental Divide. The acquisition sparked the preliminary phase of American expansion across the Mississippi, in which rugged mountain men and resolute missionaries penetrated wilderness never before seen by whites. By word of mouth, official reports, handbills, and newspaper articles, their descriptions of the West filtered back home. Restless and independent, thousands of American settlers set their sights on the West as a land of opportunity.

Within forty years of the Louisiana Purchase, the first wave of American pioneers flooded across the vast landscape.

LEWIS AND CLARK...ET AL.

Even before he finalized the Louisiana Purchase, President Thomas Jefferson commissioned Meriwether Lewis and William Clark "to explore the Missouri river, & such principle stream of it, as, by its course & communication with the waters of the Pacific Ocean, may offer the most direct and practicable water communication across this continent, for the purposes of commerce." Accompanied by about forty men, the

Meriwether Lewis

William Clark

EXPLORATIONS OF THE LOUISIANA PURCHASE

two explorers left Washington, D.C., in the summer of 1803 and spent the winter in St. Louis preparing for their journey. On May 14, 1804, the expedition started up the Missouri River. Plagued by "ticks, musquiters and knats," as Lewis noted, it took them five months to travel the 1,600 miles (2,574km) to Mandan Indian territory in North Dakota. Along the way, they established largely friendly relations with the indigenous people they met.

The party built a small winter camp, which they named Fort Mandan, and wintered at the site. While they waited out the fierce weather, they were joined by Sacagawea, a Shoshone woman. She would serve as an interpreter for the rest of the mission and would point out landmarks as they passed through Shoshone territory. The explorers left their fort in April 1805 and continued up the Missouri. In a letter to his mother, Lewis extolled the land they traversed:

This immence river we have so far ascended waters one of the fairest portions of the globe, nor do I believe that there is in the universe a similar extent of country, equally fertile, well watered, and intersected by such a number of navigable streams.

In the Rockies, the explorers abandoned their boats and with the aid of Sacagawea bought some horses from the local Indians. They made their way over the mountains, then followed the Clearwater, Snake, and Columbia rivers to the Pacific Ocean. When they sighted the sea on November 7, 1805, they became the first U.S. citizens to have traveled overland from coast to coast.

Exhausted, Lewis and Clark built a few shelters, naming their winter camp Fort Clatsop, after the Native Americans who lived at the mouth of the Columbia. The winter was a wet and hungry one, so the explorers were relieved to head home in the spring of 1806. When they reached St. Louis that fall, they astonished a nation that had given them up for dead. Their return, and the news they brought, kindled the wanderlust of other adventurers.

In the meantime, Jefferson had sent other explorers to other parts of the Louisiana territory. William Dunbar and George Hunter navigated the Washita River as far west as present-day Hot Springs, Arkansas, in 1804. In 1806, Thomas Freeman and William Sparks

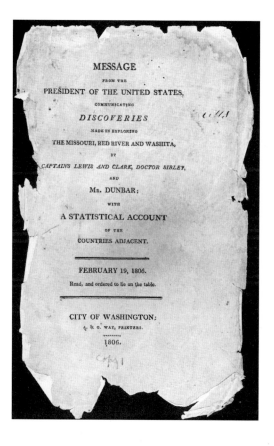

The expedition of Lewis and Clark (opposite) marked the plains Indians' discovery of whites (above left), although President Jefferson preferred to announce that it was the whites who had discovered the plains Indians (above right).

followed the course of the Red River until they met up with hostile Spaniards near Texas.

Next to Lewis and Clark's undertaking, the most important expedition of the period was the one led by Zebulon Montgomery Pike in 1806. The previous year, he had trekked north from St. Louis to Minnesota, where he encountered British fur traders from Canada. Now Jefferson sent him to explore the region between the Arkansas and Red rivers. From St. Louis, Pike crossed Osage and Pawnee country, warning the uneasy Indians that "the warriors of his Great American Father were not women to be turned back by words."

He followed the Arkansas River from the Great Bend to Royal Gorge, crossing in and out of Mexico as he traveled. The Spanish forced him out of their territory, but not before Pike observed that Mexico was a ready market for American goods. Heading north, he established a fort at Pueblo, Colorado (where he tried to scale the peak that now bears his name). He later described his trip in his book, *Journal of Western Exploration*, introducing Americans to the potential of trade in the Southwest.

The money and energy devoted to western exploration troubled Congressman Daniel Webster, who could not understand the growing fascination with a region Pike called a "great American desert." In his famous "Wasteland Speech," Webster implored his fellow legislators:

What do we want with this vast, worthless area—this region of savages and wild beasts, of deserts, of shifting sands and whirlwinds of dust and prairie dogs? To what use do we hope to put this great desert and all these endless mountain ranges?

Unlike Webster, however, many Americans had grand ideas about the uses to which the West could be put. A few were already striking out for parts unknown.

THE MOUNTAIN MEN

When Lewis and Clark returned from their expedition, they told of friendly Indians, plentiful water routes, and hunting grounds abounding with beaver. Along with the activities of British fur traders from Canada, the news caught the attention of American trappers and businessmen. Traders rushed to St. Louis to launch long trips into the northern Rockies in search of beaver pelts. Among the first of these mountain men was John Colter, a member of the Lewis and Clark expedition who became so excited by the possibilities of the fur trade that he got permission from the explorers to leave the expedition and join a band of trappers. Colter ranged through the Grand Tetons and Yellowstone country trading with the Crow, enjoying a few profitable seasons before being captured by a band of Blackfoot. A historian later recorded Colter's account of the 1808 incident:

The Indians stripped Colter stark naked.... They decided that Colter should run for his life.... A chief led him out a hundred yards in front of the crowd, pointed across the plain in the direction of the Madison River, and made a gesture for him to go....Away across the flat prairie, five miles wide between the Jefferson and Madison rivers, sped Colter toward the latter stream.... Surely a stranger sight the wild prairies never saw—this lone, naked man pursued by a pack of howling savages.... His breath was almost gone, his strength was failing, and splashes of blood blew out from his mouth and nostrils. He paused and looked around, and to his dismay he saw that one

Adopting the snowshoe and other technology from the Indians (above), Zebulon Pike (opposite, inset) explored a large tract of the Rockies, finally sighting the snowcapped peak that bears his name (opposite).

LIEUT.
Z.M.PIKE

solitary Indian was close upon him...making a desperate lunge at Colter. Colter seized the spear shaft near the head, and...stabbing the Indian to death, he took the spearhead and resumed his flight.... The crowd behind...came on like a "legion of devils," as Colter put it, howling and gesticulating with rage. But Colter was again too much for them.... His quick eye discovered near at hand an asylum of refuge in the form of a huge beaver house on the [river] bank.... Diving into the water, he made for the house

and found an entrance large enough for his body. He climbed into the upper story and was soon sitting high and dry.... He remained under cover until dark when, beaver-like, he ventured forth.

Undeterred by or unaware of Colter's Blackfoot adventure, hundreds of traders and trappers soon roamed throughout the region in search of richer beaver streams and more isolated Indian groups that would sell pelts cheaper than experienced Indians would. Some of these mountain men operated independently, while others worked for John Jacob Astor's American Fur Company (founded in 1808), Manuel Lisa's Missouri Fur Company (organized in 1809), or other organizations. From Canada, British companies such as the Hudson's Bay Company and the Northwest Company pushed into the American Rockies and the Pacific Northwest. British traders forced the Americans out of the Northwest during the War of 1812, but the Americans gained control of the mountains.

In 1824, a Canadian trader named Peter Skene Ogden led seventy-five trappers on the Snake Country Expedition to the Great Basin, where they came upon "a large Lake of 100 miles in length." This was the first sighting of the Great Salt Lake by a non-Indian. The same year, explorer and mountain man Jedediah Strong Smith made his first foray for an organization owned by Andrew Henry and William Henry Ashley. Smith's first move was to chart the South Pass through the Rocky Mountains to the unexploited, beaver-rich Green River of western Wyoming and eastern Utah. Then, in 1826, he crossed the deserts and mountains to reach Spanish California, learning about trails across Utah, Nevada, and Arizona. Next, Smith explored the Pacific coastline up to Vancouver and in 1829 crossed the Rockies to the Grand Tetons. By the time a marauding band of Comanches killed him on the Santa Fe Trail in 1831, Smith had greatly expanded American knowledge of the West.

Meanwhile, along the Green River, Ashley sent 150 trappers into the wilderness to operate on their own for a year. The next summer, he and the trappers rendezvoused at Henry's Fork to exchange furs for goods and supplies that Ashley brought from St. Louis. The trader collected so many pelts at this single gathering—about half a ton (0.5t)—that he retired a rich man.

The mountain men of the American West often spent years at a time in the wilderness. Their only possessions were those items that could be carried on horseback.

Impressed with Ashley's success, other companies soon adopted the rendezvous system, creating a generation of intrepid mountain men in the West. Often living entirely alone for months at a time, these men spent each year trapping and trading with Indians for fur. At the summer rendezvous, they emerged from the woods and gathered to trade, drink, gossip, gamble, and brawl. The rendezvous became legendary, each attracting hundreds of mountain men, Indians, and traders. After a week or two of debauchery, the mountain men returned to the wilderness for another year, and the traders went east to reap profits as high as 2,000 percent.

Mountain men such as Hugh Glass, George Yount, Thomas Fitzpatrick, and James Pattie faced Indian antagonism, grizzly-bear attacks, frostbite, dehydration, and starvation in their quest for beaver pelts. They improvised ingenious survival techniques and adopted many Indian practices in their daily life. Some married Indian women, while others were embarrassed by offers of female hospitality from friendly Indians. The image of the mountain man lives on in a description written by historian Francis Parkman, who met his first mountain men outside Bent's Fort, halfway between St. Louis and Santa Fe:

Transporting bales of skins to market in spring, white trappers sometimes fell prey to raiding Indians.

As we lay smoking round the fire after supper, we saw through the dusk three men approaching from the direction of the fort. They rode up and seated themselves near us on the ground. The foremost was a tall, well-formed man, with a face and manner such as inspire confidence at once. He wore a broad hat of felt, slouching and tattered, and the rest of his attire consisted of a frock and leggins of buckskin, rubbed with the yellow clay found among the mountains. At the heel of one moccasin was buckled a huge iron spur, with a rowel five or six inches in diameter. His horse, which stood quietly looking over his head, had a rude Mexican saddle, covered with a shaggy bear-skin, and furnished with a pair of wooden stirrups of preposterous size.

Built in 1833, Bent's Fort, complete with billiards room, dining room, blacksmith shop, and insulated ice room, was the major trading center between St. Louis and Santa Fe. Fur-trade profits began to decline around 1840, but the fort remained an important stopover for traders traveling to and from Mexico. In 1822, William Becknell charted the course of the old French trading route known as the Santa Fe Trail across the Cimarron Desert between Santa Fe and Independence, Missouri. About that time, American trappers started operating around Taos and along the Gila River.

From 1830 to 1844, caravans of huge Conestoga wagons pulled by teams of five or six oxen traveled south along the trail toward newly independent Mexico, which welcomed American trade. Loaded with up

Left: In 1834, Jason Lee (top) led five Methodists to Oregon Country where they established the first American farming village in the Willamette Valley. At the same time, Presbyterian minister Samuel Parker (bottom) was appointed by the reigning missionary council to go to Oregon and spread the word of God. Above: The first Methodist mission established in Oregon was a simple affair.

themselves for the fête.... Round the room groups of New Mexicans lounge...scowling with jealous eyes at the more favoured mountaineers.... Each [mountaineer], round his waist, wears his mountain-belt and scalp-knife, ominous of the company he is in, and some have pistols sticking in their belt. The dances—save the mark!—are without form or figure, at least those in which the white hunters sport the "fantastic toe." Seizing his partner round the waist with the gripe of the grizzly bear, each mountaineer whirls and twirls, jumps and stamps.... The hunters have the floor all to themselves.

to 2 tons (1.8t) of merchandise each, the wagons traded their way down to Santa Fe. Trade with Mexico remained strong until 1844, when the border was closed to Americans as the Mexican-American War loomed.

The arrival of Americans in a Mexican village always caused a stir. One observer described such an arrival in the following way:

> *No sooner was it known that Los Americanos had arrived, than...the sala [room] of the Alcalde [mayor] Don Cornelio Vegil...was put in order; a general invitation was distributed; and all the dusky beauties...were soon engaged in arraying*

TOWARD OREGON

As favorable reports of conditions in the Pacific Northwest—also called Oregon Country or Oregon Territory—appeared in the East, various business and church groups began to show an interest in settling the region. Around 1830, a Boston entrepreneur named Hall Jackson Kelley formed the American Society for Encouraging the Settlement of Oregon Territory. He tried but failed to enlist investors for his venture, but his activities raised the interest of another Boston businessman, Nathaniel Joseph Wyeth. In 1832, Wyeth sent a ship to sail around Cape Horn to the mouth of the Columbia, while he struck out across the continent with thirty-one men. Mountain man William Sublette guided the group partway to the West Coast along the route that would later be known as

White missionaries worked hard to convert Native Americans to Protestantism, but many Indians viewed the Christian god as only one of many "great spirits."

sions of an encounter with some Nez Percé and Flathead: "The oldest chief arose and said he was old and did not expect to know much more...but his heart was made glad, very glad, to see what he had never seen before...a minister of the Gospel." Parker returned east the following year, 1836, as Whitman headed west with his wife and another missionary couple. Each couple set up a missionary station in Oregon; their children were the first white Americans born there.

Before long, the American Board sent more Protestants west to set up missions. Catholic missionaries arrived from Canada, and one Belgian Jesuit, Pierre Jean de Smet, made sixteen trips to the region between 1840 and 1846. Even the mountain men were impressed by de Smet. Kit Carson wrote:

> I can say of him that if ever there was a man that wished to be good, he is one. He never feared danger...when danger required his presence among the savages and if his good works on the earth are rewarded hereafter, I am confident that his share of glory and happiness in the next life will be great.

For his part, de Smet had accurate forebodings concerning Oregon's future:

> This great territory will hold an immense population, destined to form several great and flourishing States. But then what will become of the Indians...who have possessed it from time immemorial? This, indeed, is a thorny question awakening gloomy ideas in the observer's mind.

the Oregon Trail. On his second trip to the Northwest, Wyeth built Fort William at the mouth of the Willamette River, but suspicious Hudson's Bay Company traders made sure that nothing came of the enterprise.

Missionary activity in Oregon started with the 1833 publication in the *Christian Advocate and Journal* of a letter from one William Walker. Published on the East Coast, the journal was the creation of fervent would-be missionaries who hoped to raise public interest in their plans for Oregon. The letter, which proved to be fictitious, gave an embellished description of an actual visit by three Nez Percé and one Flathead Indian to St. Louis in 1831. Walker falsely reported that the Indians had traveled a great distance to ask for the "Book of Heaven"—the Bible. East Coast Christians rushed to satisfy the Indians' imagined hunger for conversion. Among them was a group of five Methodists led west by Jason Lee in 1834. They established the first American farming community in the Willamette Valley; twenty more Methodists joined them in 1837 and fifty more in 1839.

The American Board of Commissioners for Foreign Missions, meanwhile, appointed Presbyterian minister Samuel Parker and Dr. Marcus Whitman to spread the word of God in Oregon. Parker preceded Whitman to the West Coast, along the way recording his impres-

Missionary activity drew the first lay settlers to the Willamette Valley before 1840. Along with John Charles Frémont, Kit Carson marked the Oregon Trail, demonstrating to other potential settlers that the trip west could be made without great hardship. Suddenly, "Oregon Fever" swept across the nation. The white settlement of the American West was about to begin in earnest.

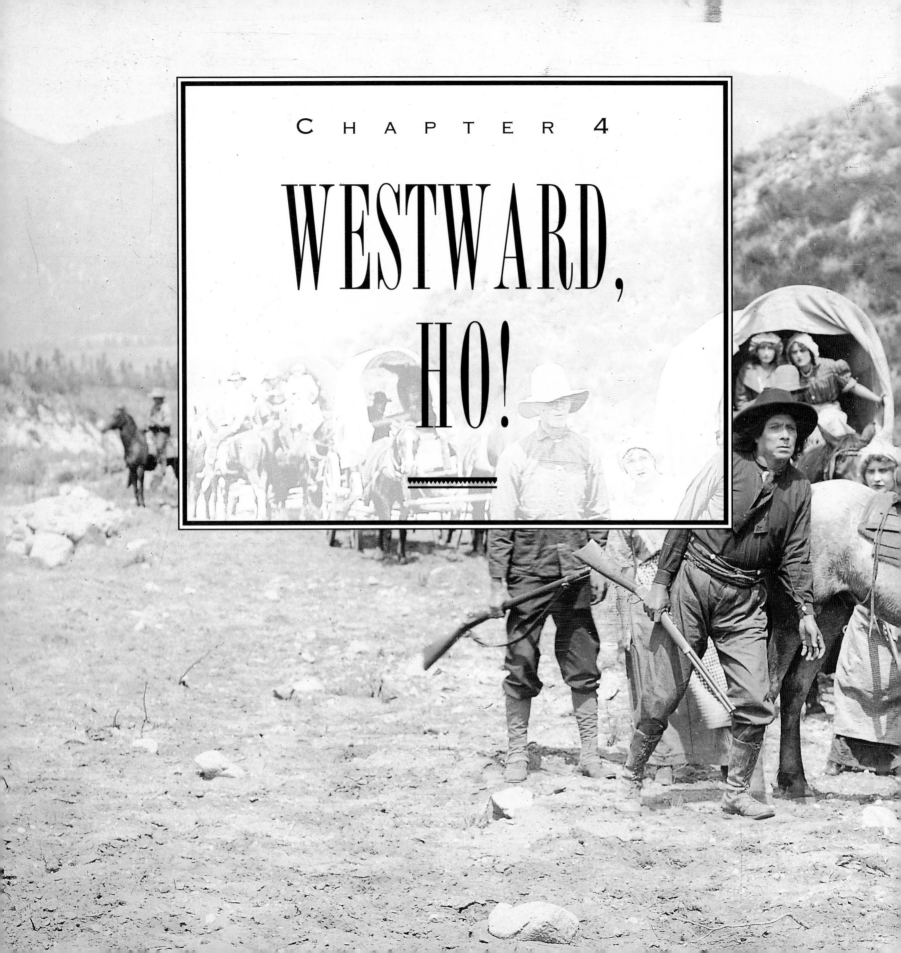

CHAPTER 4

WESTWARD, HO!

WORD SENT HOME BY THE FIRST WHITE SETTLERS IN OREGON COUNTRY EXCITED MANY EASTERN-ERS ABOUT THE POTENTIAL OF NORTH AMERICA'S FAR WEST. TRAVELERS SUCH AS JOHN CHARLES FRÉMONT AND KIT CARSON DESCRIBED ROLLING HILLS, PRISTINE LAKES AND RIVERS, LUXURIANT FORESTS, AND FERTILE PLAINS TEEMING WITH WILDLIFE. ONE PIONEER, OVERTON JOHNSON, REPORTED THAT IN THE FAR WEST, "THE FARMER'S STOCK CAN LIVE WELL ALL WINTER.... AND THERE IS NOT ONLY IN THE TERRITORY OF OREGON, BUT ALSO IN THE PROVINCE OF CALIFORNIA, ANOTHER GREAT ADVANTAGE, THAT IS, INDEED, PARAMOUNT TO ALL OTHERS: WHICH IS, HEALTH."

United States across North America was "as much a law of nature...as that the Mississippi should flow into the sea." Twenty-six years later, a New York journalist referred to this idea as "Manifest Destiny," coining a phrase that would become a touchstone of American history. For the rest of the nineteenth century, Americans moved west in fulfillment of this "destiny." Native-born pioneers were joined by immigrants from around the globe, who came to call themselves Americans as well.

Even before the mass migration started, European disease carried by white traders and missionaries devastated many of the West's indigenous peoples. During the 1820s and 1830s, epidemics wiped out large numbers of Indians in Oregon Country and along the upper Missouri River. Depopulation opened large areas of land to white incursion, fortifying white Americans' faith in Manifest Destiny. By 1840, the first American pioneers settled in the Willamette Valley. They established productive farms and raised thriving herds of cattle brought up from California. Soon, Americans

With these reports, Oregon Fever struck the United States, prodding eager farmers and would-be adventurers to risk all and journey westward to make their fortune—or simply to make a new life. In the late 1830s, many Mississippi River towns—on what was then considered the nation's western frontier—formed "Oregon Societies" to organize trips west. Most pioneers headed for the verdant coast, but Brigham Young sought a new home for his Mormon flock in the unlikely environs of the Great Basin. Like the other pioneers, the Mormons dreamed of a prosperous life in the West, but first and foremost they hoped to establish an independent community isolated from the wickedness and cruelty of the non-Mormon "Gentiles."

Almost as soon as they won their independence from Britain, Americans thought of the entire continent as their own. In 1819, Secretary of State John Quincy Adams stated that the expansion of the

living in Oregon petitioned the federal government for official help in buttressing their claim to the land. They were worried by trappers and traders from British Canada's Hudson's Bay Company, who operated throughout the area and claimed possession of the territory in dispute.

White American settlers moved west on a network of roads and trails that over time grew from rough footpaths to major highways. Some, such as the Santa Fe Trail (from Independence to Santa Fe) and the Old Spanish Trail (from Santa Fe to Los Angeles), were well established by the 1840s. Others, such as the Oregon Trail (from Independence to the Columbia River) and the Mormon Trail (from Illinois to the Great Salt Lake), would become major corridors in a few short years. Still others appeared later, including the Central Overland Route (from Nebraska to California) and the California Trail (from Idaho to California).

A steady stream of westward-bound wagon trains started in the 1840s and swelled with each passing year, until the railroad replaced them as the preferred mode of pioneer travel.

OREGON FEVER

As Oregon Fever set in, wagon trains poured into Oregon Country. The 2,100-mile (3,319km) trip took six months to complete, but Americans made the trek by the thousands. Dr. Elijah White led the first train of 112 people and sixteen wagons across the Oregon Trail in 1842. The following year, Peter H. Burnett organized about a thousand people for the journey. When he heard about Burnett's plans, newspaperman Horace Greeley declared that "this migration of more than a thousand persons in one body to Oregon wears an aspect of insanity." But the pioneers made it to the Northwest with five thousand cattle. Their feat was soon called the "great migration." Excited by the news of this success, another fifteen hundred pioneers surged west in 1844. Twice as many arrived in 1845; by 1852, the flow reached fifteen thousand. The early wagon trains consisted of perhaps twenty-five or thirty families, while later trains might boast as many as two hundred wagons.

Because it cost a family about five hundred dollars to make the trip to Oregon, most of the emigrants came from the middle class. Prosperous farmers, lawyers, merchants, and tradesmen faced the privations of crossing arid plains and treacherous rivers. Along with their wives and children, they endured backbreaking toil and primitive living conditions unlike anything many of them had experienced before.

For the most part, the pioneers had few run-ins with Native Americans living along the route, who were generally more interested in trading with or simply meeting the strangers. As the flow of travelers increased, however, the Indians came to resent the intruders. In the late 1840s, the U.S. Army built forts along the Oregon Trail to provide protection for the pioneers.

Traveling without the benefit of road signs, sometimes on a trail barely distinguishable from its surroundings, the pioneers relied on various landmarks to guide them along the Oregon Trail. For the first two days out of Independence, they followed the Santa Fe Trail. They then turned northeast at the Kansas River and covered 150 miles (241km) to

reach Fort Kearney on the Platte River in Nebraska. Following that river and its north fork for 300 miles (483km), the pioneers crossed dry country to Fort Laramie in southeastern Wyoming. From there, it took them ten more days along the North Platte to reach Independence Rock, after which they followed the Sweetwater River into the Rocky Mountains. South Pass took them across the Continental Divide; they then turned southwest to reach Fort Bridger in southwestern Wyoming. From here, the wagon trains headed northwest along the Bear River to Fort Hall in the Tetons. Following the Snake River past Fort Boise, they crossed the Blue Mountains, where the Snake drains into the Columbia River. Pioneers then followed the Columbia west to the Willamette River.

Most of the settlers ended their journey in the Willamette Valley. Before they did, however, many stopped at the mission station of Dr. Marcus Whitman near Fort Walla Walla for much-needed medical attention after the rigors of their journey. The generous aid they received there would be repeated by other settlers when they reached their final destination. Frémont described the spirit of mutual assistance that he witnessed among the settlers in Oregon Country:

> Others have already crossed the river into their land of promise—the Willamette Valley. Others were daily arriving; and all of them had been furnished with shelter, so far as it could be afforded.... Necessary clothing and provisions (the latter to be afterwards returned in kind from the produce of their labor) were also furnished. This friendly assistance was of great value to the emigrants, whose families were otherwise exposed to much suffering in the winter rains.

In their new home, this cooperative attitude enabled the settlers to prosper. Living in disputed territory far from "the states," these Americans were left to govern themselves. Around 1841, a rudimentary democratic government began to take form; this system evolved according to the changing needs of the rapidly growing community. Its first priority was to present a strong American front to the Hudson's Bay Company, which claimed the region on behalf of Britain. The territorial conflict was resolved in 1846, when the United States and Britain signed a treaty that defined the forty-ninth parallel as the border between Oregon Country and British North America.

To the south, a smaller stream of American pioneers flowed into California, which at the time was claimed by Mexico. These settlers arrived via various turnoffs from the Oregon Trail, one of which was made famous by a doomed wagon train that set out in 1846. Headed by the brothers George and Jacob Donner, the eighty-nine-member caravan was racked by disagreements from the start. They fell badly behind schedule in their effort to reach their destination before winter. At Fort Bridger, the Donner party decided to leave the Oregon Trail and shorten their journey by taking a route known as Hastings' Cutoff. They read about the route in a guidebook written by one Lansford

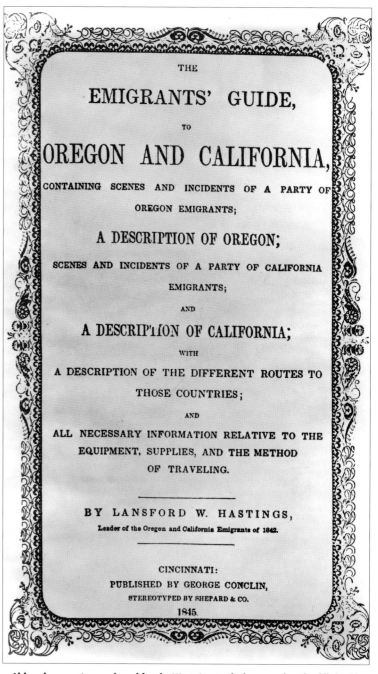

THE

EMIGRANTS' GUIDE,

TO

OREGON AND CALIFORNIA,

CONTAINING SCENES AND INCIDENTS OF A PARTY OF OREGON EMIGRANTS;

A DESCRIPTION OF OREGON;

SCENES AND INCIDENTS OF A PARTY OF CALIFORNIA EMIGRANTS;

AND

A DESCRIPTION OF CALIFORNIA;

WITH

A DESCRIPTION OF THE DIFFERENT ROUTES TO THOSE COUNTRIES;

AND

ALL NECESSARY INFORMATION RELATIVE TO THE EQUIPMENT, SUPPLIES, AND THE METHOD OF TRAVELING.

BY LANSFORD W. HASTINGS,
Leader of the Oregon and California Emigrants of 1842.

CINCINNATI:
PUBLISHED BY GEORGE CONCLIN,
STEREOTYPED BY SHEPARD & CO.
1845.

Although many pioneers bound for the West Coast relied on travel guides filled with dangerous misinformation and colorful fantasy, most managed to find their way and start a new life.

been forced to abandon most of their wagons. They did not reach the eastern foothills of the Sierras until October 23, very late in the traveling season. Nonetheless, they believed they could make it over the mountains before winter set in.

As the Donner party struggled through the mountains, a fierce early storm stranded them in deep snow. They built a few cabins for shelter, but food was running low. A small group tried but failed to make their way across a final pass. Later, another fifteen volunteers were sent out to get help. In the cold and snow, their supplies quickly ran out; the volunteers survived only by eating the remains of four who died. Conditions were no better in the base camp. All the food was gone by mid-December, reducing the pioneers to a diet of leather and bones. According to one survivor of that brutal winter,

> The families shared with one another as long as they had anything to share. Each one's portion was very small. The hides [of the last cattle] were boiled, and the bones were burned brown and eaten. We tried to eat a decayed buffalo robe, but it was too tough, and there was no nourishment in it. Some of the few mice that came into camp were caught and eaten.

Eventually, the living had no choice but to eat those who had died of hunger. When help finally arrived, only small rescue parties could make it over the mountains from Sutter's Fort. Each could bring only a small amount of food and carry out only a few survivors at a time. By the time the rescue was completed, in February 1847, only forty-nine of the original party were left. One rescuer recorded the harrowing scene at the camp:

> Near the principal cabins I saw bodies entire, with the exception that the abdomens had been cut open and the entrails extracted. Their flesh had either been wasted by famine or evaporated by exposure to the dry atmosphere, and they presented the appearance of mummies. Strewn around the cabins were dislocated and broken skulls (in some instances sawed asunder with care, for the purpose of extracting the brains), human skeletons, in short, in every variety of mutilation. A more revolting and appalling spectacle I never witnessed.

Groups of travelers who reached the mountains late in the season, such as the Donner party, often had to abandon their possessions if they hoped to cross the snowy passes.

Hastings, who, in fact, had never actually traversed the shortcut. Hastings, who was busy guiding another wagon train west, failed to mark the cutoff as he had promised Donner he would, and the Donner Party was forced to blaze its own trail.

Traveling across barren and rugged terrain, the Donner party frequently went off course, causing further delays and tensions. One member, John Reed, was exiled to the wilderness for killing another man with a knife. As their supplies ran low, they sent an advance party ahead to Sutter's Fort in California. One of the scouts returned with some provisions, mules and two Indian guides, but by then Indian raiders had stolen thirty head of the party's cattle and the pioneers had

James Reed

James Clyman

Leanna Donner

Stranded in the foothills of the Sierras, the Donner party was not equipped for a winter in the mountains. Trees chopped for firewood in snow six feet deep left tall stumps when spring arrived (below). Left: The survivors of the Donner party fiasco included party leader James Reed, explorer James Clyman, and Leanna Donner, who was thirteen years old at the time of the tragedy.

Between the Mississippi River Valley and the West Coast, indigenous Americans watched hordes of white settlers pass by on their way to Oregon and California.

dent convinced Congress that the U.S. citizens living in the region were in need of protection, and Oregon was made a full-fledged territory of the United States.

Of course, not all was misery and death on the frontier. The settlers discovered that some of the reports that had drawn them west were exaggerated, but they also found that Oregon Country did indeed offer ample wonders. In a letter home, one woman described an 1852 New Year's Day party in Columbia City:

> Well We had Rosted Ducks...And Fat Chickens and Rosted pig and Sausages And green Apl pie And Mince pies and Custard pies And Cakes of difrent kindes [and] Inglish goosburyes And Plums Blue And green gages And Siberian crab Apples And oregon Apples.... I never Saw Sutch Black Buryes And Ras Bryes As There Is in this Countrey in All My Life Time.

Another settler described the pleasures of life in that frontier town:

> [The theatre] is very amusing. They have good musick. The infaintry brass band plays in the theatre...every wednesday knight they act. Last Tuesday night when [the ship] came rolling in the peopel were all in the theatre and as soon as she fired the cannon it roused all the people out of the theatre and they all charged out and the actors had to stop their peices on the stage until some of them come back.... Out of a hundred they had no more than a dosen left in the theatre.

The forty-nine survivors, including some members of the Donner family, enjoyed (or suffered) some notoriety in subsequent years.

Travelers who managed to reach Oregon or California still faced danger from Indians, accidents, or disease. Among the casualties were Dr. Whitman and his mission at Fort Walla Walla. In 1847, a measles epidemic struck the surrounding area, killing a number of whites and far more Indians. Certain that the doctor was either poisoning them with his medicine or reserving his real medicine for white settlers, a band of Cayuse raided the mission and killed many residents, including Dr. Whitman. A few of the settlers escaped, and about fifty women and children were captured. A Hudson's Bay Company trader, Peter Skene Ogden, successfully negotiated the release of the captives, but the inci-

THE MORMONS

One group of pioneers looked west in search of heavenly rather than earthly rewards. These were the Mormons, members of the Church of Jesus Christ of Latter-day Saints, who sought to build an independent community far from the temptations and travails of worldly civilization. Founded in 1830 by Joseph Smith, the church moved from New York to Ohio and then to Missouri, looking for a place where they could follow their beliefs free of persecution. Their belief in the prophecies and principles recorded by Smith in *The Book of Mormon*, as well as their desire to found a government headed by supposedly divine Mormon

Joseph Smith (left) led his Mormon followers on a search for a permanent home until some of them murdered him (above) for advocating polygamy.

leaders, outraged mainstream Christians. As the group grew, tensions with its gentile neighbors increased; mutual intolerance sometimes sparked violence. The governor of Missouri finally concluded that "the Mormons must be treated as enemies and must be exterminated or driven from the state, if necessary, for the public peace."

The church moved on to Illinois and founded the town of Nauvoo, which soon became the state's largest city, with a population of fifteen thousand. But in 1844, when Smith started advocating polygamy for church leaders, his opponents murdered him. A group of Mormons who rejected polygamy moved on to Michigan; the rest stayed in Nauvoo and selected Brigham Young as their new leader. In 1846, Young ordered the Mormons to prepare for a move westward, where they would build a new Zion. As the site for this settlement, he chose an isolated area west of Colorado and south of Wyoming, deep in the heart of the forbidding Great Basin. He hoped that there the Mormons could establish their own republic, free of outside interference.

Young planned the venture carefully. He first led a 148-person, seventy-three-wagon "Pioneer Band" to scout the route, build base camps for the travelers, and plant crops along the way to feed them.

The efficient system allowed twelve thousand Mormons to join Young at the Missouri River by fall. Wintering at the site, the pioneers established friendly relations with the Indians. In the spring of 1847, Young set out with the Pioneer Band to scout the next leg of the journey. Blazing a trail north of the Platte River in order to avoid the Oregon Trail to the south, the party ignored the warnings they heard at Fort Bridger and took Hastings' Cutoff. When they reached the site of Salt Lake City, on July 24, 1847, Orson Pratt recalled:

> We called camp together, and it fell to my lot to offer up prayer and thanksgiving in behalf of our company, all of whom had been preserved from the Missouri River to this point; and, after dedicating ourselves to the land and to the Lord, and imploring his blessings upon our labours, we appointed various committees to attend to different branches of business, preparatory to putting in crops, and in about two hours of our arrival we began to plough, and the same afternoon built a dam to irrigate the soil, which at the spot where we were ploughing was exceedingly dry.

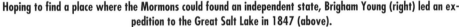

Hoping to find a place where the Mormons could found an independent state, Brigham Young (right) led an expedition to the Great Salt Lake in 1847 (above).

Irrigation was crucial to the Mormons' success; it allowed them to turn parched plains into fertile farmland. The crops planted that summer, though, could barely feed the first contingent of eighteen hundred settlers who arrived before winter. The following year, a swarm of grasshoppers descended on the crops and ate most of them before a flock of seagulls appeared and ate the grasshoppers—an event the Mormons considered miraculous. Despite the setbacks, Young urged more settlers to "come immediately and prepare to go West, bringing with you all kinds of choice seeds, grains, vegetables, fruits, shrubbery, trees and vines—anything that will please the eye, gladden the heart or cheer the soul of man."

The population of Deseret, as the settlement was called, doubled in 1848. Again, there was not enough food that winter, a season the pioneers called the "Starving Time." Undeterred, Young meticulously laid out plans for a city and established a policy of communal land ownership under which each settler was assigned as much land as he needed. Through careful control of water use, unity of purpose, and joint effort, the Mormons carved a successful community out of seemingly barren

terrain. Their fortunes improved when the California gold rush started in 1849, for many wagon trains passed through Mormon country on their way to the gold fields. The Mormons exchanged provisions for manufactured goods from the east, often at prices the travelers considered outrageously expensive.

In 1848, at the end of the Mexican War, Mexico ceded territory that included Mormon country to the United States. Congress designated the region Utah Territory in 1850, and President Millard Fillmore named Young its governor. Governed according to Young's principles, the Mormon settlement grew as thousands of European converts arrived. The years 1856 through 1860 saw the arrival of the Handcart Companies, groups of up to three hundred people who pushed or pulled rickshaw-like carts to Deseret. A total of three thousand Mormons traveled west this way, which was far cheaper than wagon travel. By 1856, there were twenty-two thousand Mormons in Deseret.

Essentially a theocracy with Young as its dictator, Utah Territory hardly seemed like a U.S. possession. In response to complaints of discrimination against non-Mormons, twenty-five hundred

Government troops marched west in 1857 to enforce federal policy. Fearing oppression or even expulsion, the Mormons repelled the soldiers; a group of vengeful Mormons then killed 120 gentile pioneers in the Mountain Meadows Massacre. Eager to avoid outright war, the United States finally convinced the Mormons of its peaceful and tolerant intentions. A non-Mormon governor was installed, but Young remained the true leader of the territory until he died.

BY WAGON TRAIN

Between the laughing and the crying,
The living and the dying,
The singing and the sighing,
The wheels roll west.

—Trail Song

Wherever they were headed, pioneer wagon trains employed tried-and-true methods to increase the odds of success. Before getting under way, each train elected a captain and drafted a set of rules to be followed on the trail. Most important matters were decided democratically, by council, thus keeping conflict to a minimum. Guided by experienced mountain men, wagon-train pioneers frequently referred to guidebooks of varying reliability for information on routes, landmarks, and survival techniques. Smaller than the Conestogas, their wagons had beds measuring about 10 by 4 by 2 feet (3m by 1.2 by 0.6m) and were pulled by teams of six oxen or mules. Awkward and top-heavy, the wagons offered rough riding and overturned frequently.

To keep the weight of the wagons down, pioneers were advised not to take furniture or other items not essential to survival. Those who did almost always discarded their excess freight as the trail got tougher. Among the first things to be discarded were fancy women's dresses, which Native Americans often picked up and wore themselves; as one observer reported: "Worn without regard to age or sex, they were a costume picture only a trifle more fantastic than the emigrants themselves." Other items, such as tools, basic household articles, and sturdy clothing, were standard equipment for a covered wagon, as well as provisions. Each adult required 150 pounds (68kg) of flour, 5 pounds (2.3kg) of baking soda, 10 pounds (4.5kg) of jerky, and 40 pounds (18kg) each of bacon, dried fruit, sugar, and coffee. Rice, yeast, vinegar, and molasses were also brought along.

Many pioneers relied on oxen, which are stronger and hardier than horses, to pull their covered wagons west. Once the settlers arrived, they could use the animals to pull plows.

Wagon trains started their trips in the spring in order to complete the journey by fall. On the trail, travelers typically woke at 4 A.M. to get moving by 7 A.M. Trains generally paused for ten minutes each hour to rest the livestock; at about 11 A.M., they stopped for "nooning." By 2 P.M., after chores, a meal, and perhaps some rest, pioneers returned to the trail and pressed on as long as they could, sometimes well into the night. To cross deep rivers, they removed the wheels from their wagons and floated them to the opposite bank. Two or more teams might be hitched to a wagon and assisted by men, women, and children to pull it through mud or up a steep trail. Faced with searing heat, violent storms, scarce water, and meager grazing land, the trains covered an average of 15 miles (24km) a day. At night, the pioneers pulled their wagons into a circle that would provide defense in case of Indian attack. The weary travelers slept in or under their wagons, or in tents pitched within the circle.

The trip west was filled with astonishing sights for the pioneers. Catherine Haun, who made the journey in 1849, wrote of one such spectacle witnessed by her wagon train as it approached the Rockies:

> Finally after a couple weeks' travel the distant mountains of the west came into view. This was the land of the buffalo. One day a herd came in our direction like a great black cloud, a threatening moving mountain, advancing toward us very swiftly and with wild snorts, noses almost to the ground and tails flying in midair. I haven't any idea how many there were but they seemed to be innumerable and made a deafening terrible noise. As is their habit, when stampeding, they did not turn out of their course for anything. Some of our wagons were within their line

Poorly marked and incomplete trails sometimes led wagon trains to the edge of a cliff, where wagons and animals had to be lowered down the side with winches (top). The long and rugged journey west pushed some oxen and horses beyond exhaustion (above).

of advance and in consequence one was completely demolished and two were overturned. Several persons were hurt, one child's shoulder being dislocated, but fortunately no one was killed.

Unfortunately, injury, illness, and death were the pioneers' constant companions on the trail. Pregnant women often died in childbirth, and men suffered accidental gunshot wounds. Dysentery, altitude sickness, and cholera stalked one and all. Another common cause of death was drowning at river crossings. In a letter sent Back East, Abigail Malick, who traveled the Oregon Trail in 1850, described the drowning death of her seventeen-year-old son, Hiram:

> *Hiram drounded in [the] Plat River At the Mouth of Dear Krick. He went Aswiming with some other boys of the Compeny that we Trailed with And he swum Acrost the river and the Water run very fast And he could not reach this side. The young Men tried to save him but he [had the Cramp] And Could swim no more. And they Said o hiram do swim but he said I cannot swim eney More. And one young Man took A pole And started to him And the water ran so fast that he thought he Could not swim eney more so he returned And left him to his fate. And the other boys Called to him and said O hiram O swim. And he said o my god I cannot eney More. They said that he went down in the water seven or eight times before he drounded. And then he said o my god O lord gesus receive My Soul for I am no More. Oyes I think that if ever A young Man went to their lord gesus that he Did for he Always Was A very good boy and that [all who] knew him liked him.*

The hard journey also killed many oxen, mules, and horses. The stresses of trail life reduced some parties to bickering over petty affronts or travel strategy. Many wagon trains broke up into separate parties that went their separate ways. Still, camaraderie and solidarity usually pre-

A way station on the trails west, Salt Lake City thrived by trading with transient wagon trains.

vailed, and pioneers made it to their destination in the face of all obstacles. The enduring pioneer spirit was the stuff of many fond memories of the trail, memories that erased the suffering borne on the way west. A Fourth of July celebration described in Catherine Haun's diary captures that spirit:

> *After dinner that night it was proposed that we celebrate the day and we all heartily join[ed] in....We sang patriotic songs, repeated what little we could of the Declaration of Independence, fired off a gun or two, and gave three cheers for the United States and California Territory in particular!... The young folks decorated themselves in all manner of fanciful and grotesque costumes, Indian characters being most popular. To the rollicking music of violin and Jew's harp we danced until midnight.*

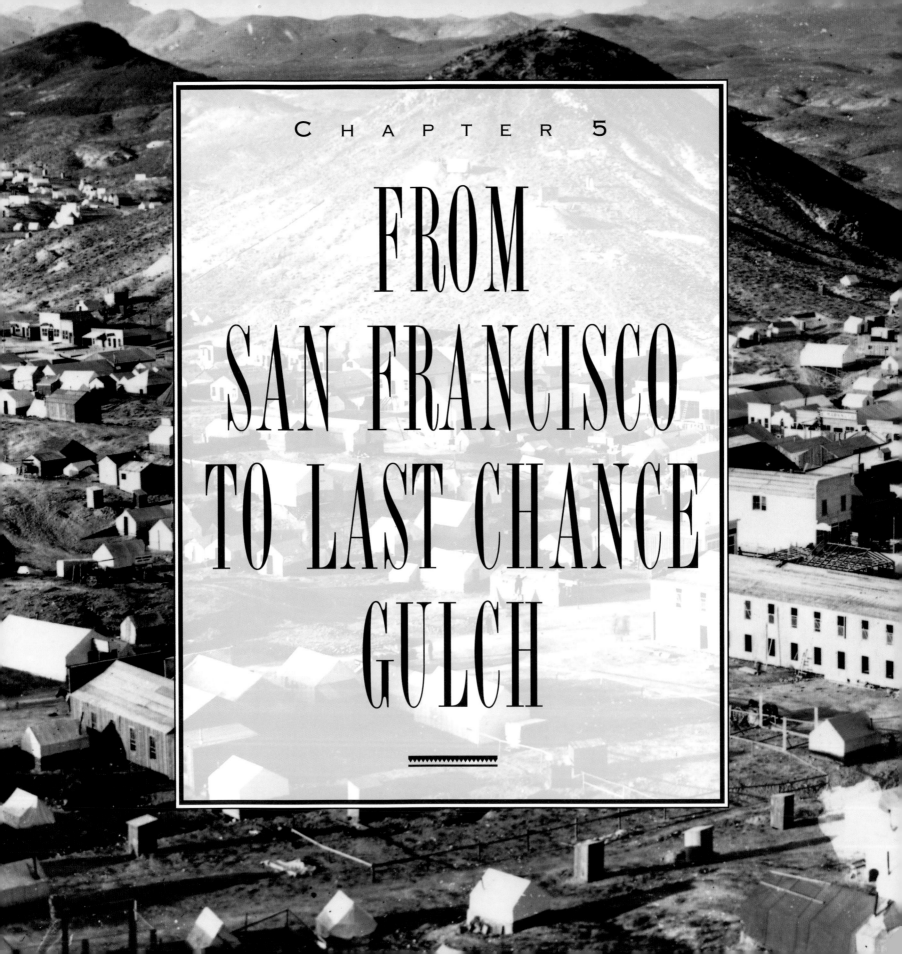

CHAPTER 5

FROM SAN FRANCISCO TO LAST CHANCE GULCH

LIKE OREGON FEVER, WHICH BROUGHT ABOUT 350,000 PIONEERS TO AMERICA'S WESTERN COASTLINE BETWEEN 1841 AND 1866, GOLD FEVER LURED HUNDREDS OF THOUSANDS MORE TO THE FAR WEST'S INTERIOR. FOR FIFTY YEARS, STARTING IN 1849, PROSPECTORS CRISSCROSSED THE REGION'S MOUNTAINS, HOPING TO STRIKE IT RICH. THEY PANNED, PICKED, TUNNELED, AND DRILLED FOR PRECIOUS METALS, SOMETIMES DISCOVERING GREAT DEPOSITS OR VEINS WORTH MILLIONS OF DOLLARS. MORE OFTEN, THOUGH, THEY WRUNG ONLY A FEW POUCHES OF SILVER OR GOLD FROM THEIR CLAIMS AND MOVED ON.

Miners swarmed to every site where a find was reported. Some strikes proved disappointing or even nonexistent, but a few yielded astonishing quantities of valuable minerals. Everywhere gold or silver was found, cities sprang up almost instantly, many disappearing just as fast when the mines were depleted. Rooming houses, restaurants, laundries, general stores, and especially saloons sprouted and withered with equal alacrity, depending on the fortunes of the prospectors. Carefully weighed out gold dust served as currency; it would ultimately be converted into cash by banks or speculators. And with gold dust circulating freely, prospectors were not the only ones getting rich. One woman who ran a boardinghouse in Nevada City, California, wrote of her huge profits:

Many a night have I shut my oven door on two milk-pans filled high with bags of gold dust and I have often slept with my mattress lined.... I must have had more than two hundred thousand dollars lying unprotected in my bedroom.

Endowed with such wealth, a number of mining settlements matured into permanent towns and cities occupied by people originally drawn west by the mining bonanza. Before long, the United States had two centers of population: the states between the Atlantic coast and the Mississippi River valley, and the territories west of the Rocky Mountains. Transit and communication between the two distant regions was slow and unreliable until the arrival of cross-country telegraph lines, express mail services, and the transcontinental railroad. Partly as a result of the mineral rushes, the nation spanned the continent in a matter of only a few years.

CALIFORNIA, HERE I COME!

Before the gold rush of 1849, California was a sleepy land of Mexican ranchers, American traders, and impoverished Indians. A Mexican possession, it was home to only about seven hundred "Anglos"—non-Mexican whites—in 1845. Far from the Mexican capitol, California was free from official intrusion in its affairs. San Francisco, then called Yerba Buena, served as an American outpost for the maritime trade in sea otter pelts and whale oil. Some Anglos traded with the rancheros for the hides and tallow produced by the cattle business.

The United States gained possession of California during the 1846–48 war with Mexico. When the war broke out, Anglo Californians became worried that they would lose their autonomy as the opposing forces asserted their claims to the region. They launched the Bear Flag Revolt, declaring the independence of the Republic of California. But the United States easily annexed California, to the indignation of Mexico. After the war, Mexico formally ceded the territory to the United States, and Congress created the Territory of California.

Deadwood in 1876

Rough-and-tumble towns sprouted wherever prospectors made a strike. Filthy and fire-prone, the settlements nonetheless provided all the miners' needs.

The great California gold rush began when workman James Marshall (top right) discovered gold at the sawmill (above) he was building for John Sutter (right).

Nine days before Mexico and the United States signed the Treaty of Guadalupe Hidalgo, a handyman named James Marshall found gold on land claimed by John Augustus Sutter. A flamboyant Swiss immigrant, Sutter had built an imposing, adobe-walled fort near Yerba Buena, from which he hoped to reign over his own republic. He hired Marshall to build a sawmill and millrace on his land; it was during this construction that Marshall made his fateful discovery on January 24, 1848. He later recalled the moment:

One morning in January—it was a clear cold morning: I shall never forget that morning—as I was taking my usual walk along the race after shutting off the water, my eye was caught with the glimpse of something shining in the bottom of the ditch. There was about a foot of water running then. I reached my hand down and picked it up; it made my heart thump, for I was certain it was gold. The piece was about half the size and of the shape of a pea. Then I saw another piece in the water.

Marshall and Sutter confirmed that the nuggets were gold and quietly applied to the local authorities for a mining lease. But news of the discovery at Sutter's Mill soon leaked out, and by June nearly every male in the vicinity of San Francisco headed for the hills. Sailors abandoned their ships and soldiers deserted their posts. One observer noted that "the farmers have thrown aside their plows, the lawyers their briefs, the doctors their pills, the priests their prayer books, and all are now digging gold."

While most of the Forty-Niners headed west by land, some traveled by ship (above). People also came from England (right) and all over the world to try their hands at prospecting.

FOR CALIFORNIA AND THE GOLD REGION DIRECT!

The Magnificent, Fast Sailing and favorite packet Ship,

JOSEPHINE,

BURTHEN 400 TONS, CAPT.

Built in the most superb manner of Live Oak, White Oak and Locust, for a New York and Liverpool Packet; thoroughly Copper-fastened and Coppered; she is a very fast sailer, having crossed the Atlantic from Liverpool to New-York in 14 days, the shortest passage ever made by a Sailing Ship. Has superior accommodations for Passengers, can take Gentlemen with their Ladies and families. Will probably reach ☞SAN FRANCISCO THIRTY DAYS ahead of any Ship sailing at the same time. Will sail about the

10th November Next.

For Freight or Passage apply to the subscriber.

RODNEY FRENCH,

New Bedford, October 15th. No. 103 North Water Street, Rodman's Wharf.

The strike at Sutter's Mill was part of a huge mother lode. One hundred twenty miles (193km) long and 6 to 8 miles (9.7–12.9km) wide, it stretched from Mariposa in the south to Downieville in the north. In the mountains above San Francisco, fortune hunters waded into mountain streams and picked or panned gold lumps and gold dust from the riverbeds. A Monterey resident wrote to his sons in Boston, "It is the opinion generally that the gold regions extend over many rivers and can not be exhausted in a hundred years. I believe there is now being taken from the sand daily ten thousand dollars.... When this will end we can not at present imagine."

Nor could Californians imagine the impact the find would have on American history. Word of the California gold craze spread to the states and around the world by the end of the year. In 1849, Americans poured west by the thousands. For the most part misinformed, badly equipped, and ill-prepared, the "Forty-Niners," as they came to be known, made the long and dangerous voyage by land or water. Some traveled overland by wagon train, others boarded ships for a sixty-day trip around Cape Horn. Many land travelers died on the way, especially in a treacherous desert spot the travelers named Death Valley. But few would-be Forty-Niners were discouraged.

More than seventeen thousand people—mostly young white men—left the East Coast for California in the first three months of 1849. The prospectors, also known as "sourdoughs" for their reliance on that type of bread as a staple, flocked to San Francisco, transforming the village into a raucous frontier city. One returning trader described the scene:

> We passed through the Golden Gate...and, landing, I saw with astonishment the great change that had come over San Francisco. The little idle place I had left...was now, by the potent power of gold, metamorphized into a canvas city of several thousand people.

Living conditions in San Francisco were primitive and prices were outrageously high. Unpaved and littered with sewage and debris, the

When ships carrying Forty-Niners arrived in San Francisco, the crews often abandoned their vessels in favor of the mines (right). Every day, hundreds of prospectors lined up at the post office hoping for word from home (below).

slippery, rutted streets challenged surefooted pedestrians and horses alike. The prospectors crowded into filthy restaurants, boardinghouses, saloons, and gambling halls, many of which were run by Chinese immigrants.

Bricks cost a dollar apiece, producing a severe housing shortage that boosted rents to eight hundred dollars per month and more. Top dollar bought, at best, a flea-infested bunk in a "hotel" with dirt floors and canvas walls. One prospector explained, "when we creep into one of these nests, it is optional with us whether we unboot or uncoat ourselves; but it would be looked upon as an act of ill-breeding to go to bed with one's hat on." Laundry charges were so high that most Forty-

Niners either shipped out their laundry to be done in Hawaii (it would be shipped back clean) or bought new clothes when their old ones became unwearable.

Still, prospective millionaires continued to arrive in droves, drawn by the vision of huge sums of money to be made. Daily wages for the most ordinary kinds of labor started at about fifteen dollars; freelance prospectors could take in fifty dollars worth of gold a day; hustlers could make money doing almost anything. Speculators could demand as much as an ounce (28.4g) of gold from mail-hungry miners eager to buy a place toward the front of the line at the post office. No one wanted to interrupt the quest for wealth for even a moment, even to receive news from home. As one visitor wrote:

> Every thing was going ahead like a race horse, or a steam locomotive.... All were in a hurry. Passing today, you would see a vacant lot, and passing again in forty-eight hours, there would be a store in which would be a large stock of goods.... As many as forty buildings have gone up in forty-eight hours.

By the end of 1849, San Francisco had twenty thousand residents and six hundred ships, most of them abandoned, rode at anchor in San Francisco Bay. An exploding population, combined with the almost complete lack of laws and law officers, soon led to a growing crime problem. In response, citizens formed vigilance committees to mete out justice. While the governor appointed by Congress stood by helplessly, vigilantes captured, tried, and punished suspected wrongdoers. In September 1849, some prominent local citizens held a constitutional convention, and on October 10 they adopted a constitution. Californians ratified the constitution that November and elected a governor and territorial legislators.

Crime did not restrict itself to the city. A letter written by a resident of a mining camp in the mountains reported, "In the short space of twenty-four days, we have had murders, fearful accidents, bloody deaths, a mob, whippings, a hanging, an attempt at suicide, and a fatal duel." Vigilante justice was the only law in the remote Sierra Nevada, where prospectors trekked from San Francisco.

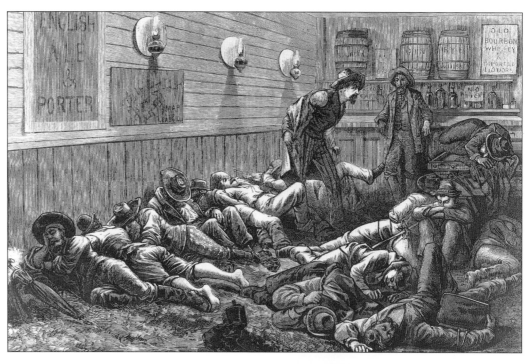

Most of the people storming the peaks, however, came not to make mischief but to make money. Louise Clappe, the wife of a prospector along Feather River, described the sourdoughs:

> *Our countrymen are the most discontented of mortals. They are always longing for "big strikes." If a "claim" is paying them a steady income, by which, if they pleased, they could lay up more in a month, than they could accumulate in a year at home, still, they are dissatisfied, and, in most cases, will wander off to search for better "diggings." There are hundreds now pursuing this foolish course, who, if they had stopped where they first "camped," would now have been rich men.... Almost all with whom we are acquainted seem to have lost. Some have had their "claims" jumped.... If a fortunate or an unfortunate (which shall I call him?) does happen to make a "big strike," he is almost sure to fall into the hands of the professed gamblers, who soon relieve him of all care of it.*

The first prospectors at a site gathered gold easily, panning and sluicing along streams or simply picking it up from the ground. To unearth more gold, they employed a technique known as placer mining,

Young men armed with pick, hoe, and pan (above) could make a fortune in the goldfields, then return to town to blow off steam in the saloons (top).

Virginia City, Nevada, located at the dizzyingly rich Comstock Lode, typified the boomtowns that spread across the West in the mining bonanza of the late 1800s.

in which they used hydraulic pressure to wash gold from the earth and separate it from the dirt. As the surface gold was exhausted, mining companies appeared with more sophisticated techniques, digging mine shafts and drilling into rock to mine the actual underground veins. Of course, the mines eventually gave out altogether, turning boom into bust. Louise Clappe observed the decline of the mines around the Feather River:

Nearly every person on the river received the same stepmother's treatment from Dame Nature, in this her mountain workshop. Of course the whole world (our world) was, to use a phrase much in vogue here, "dead broke." The shopkeepers, restaurants, and gambling houses, with an amiable confidingness peculiar to such people, had trusted the miners to that degree, that they themselves were in the same moneyless condition.

Such a batch of woeful faces was never seen before.... The mass of the unfortunates laid down the "shovel and the hoe," and left the river in crowds. It is said, that there are not twenty men remaining on Indian Bar, although, two months ago, you could count them up by hundreds.

Propelled by the prospect of boom times and certain they would not be busted, prospectors continued to stream into California. The wave of immigrants to the territory crested for four years, bringing the state's total population to 250,000 in 1852. That same year, gold production reached its peak at a total value of $81 million. By 1860, even though gold production had declined to $44 million a year, nearly 400,000 people were living in California.

TO THE MOUNTAINS

As the gold ran out in California, the prospectors ranged farther into the continent's interior. In Nevada, they discovered the Comstock Lode, a 5-mile-long (8km) and 1-mile-wide (1.6km) vein, in 1858. With this find, another prospecting rush was sparked and more boomtowns, such as Virginia City, began springing up. Life in these new towns was just as rough as it had been in San Francisco. One visitor described Virginia City in a letter home to his wife:

Of all the places on the face of the earth, I have never seen any quite so bad as Virginia City. It is perched up amongst desolate rocks and consists of several hundred tents, holes in the ground with men living in them like coyotes, frame shanties and mud hovels. The climate is perfectly frightful, and the water is so bad that hundreds are sick from drinking it. Alkali and arsenic are among the mildest ingredients found in it. The people as they

THE MINERS' FRONTIER, 1858—1875

rush about wild and frantic after silver, unwashed and unshaved as they are, with haggard and bloodshot eyes, look like the inmates of Bedlam.

Because most of the gold and silver in the Comstock Lode had to be extracted using expensive methods, large companies came to domi-

nate the mining there. Hundreds of prospectors worked for wages in deep shafts, facing deadly dangers such as cave-ins, explosions, and flooding. But the tunneling paid off. In 1873, four miners organized as the Consolidated Virginia tunneled 1,167 feet (356m) into Davidson Mountain and made the richest strike in the history of mining: a vein that earned them $200 million.

When prospectors found gold near Pike's Peak in 1858, they set off the Colorado Gold Rush. Greatly exaggerated rumors of the strike's potential soon reached the East and West coasts, and 100,000 Fifty-Niners rushed to the region in the spring of 1859. But extracting gold was expensive work that required great skill; by midsummer, half of those who had arrived in wagons bearing the slogan "Pike's Peak or Bust!" changed their motto to "Busted, by God!" and went home. Ironically, it was a "pre-Bust" visit to the Pike's Peak camps that inspired Horace Greeley to coin the phrase "Go West, Young Man, Go West."

Coarse and crude in the field (above), the miner's life gradually assumed some polish in town (right), where the wealth of the mineral rushes accumulated.

THE ILLUSTRATED

MINERS' HAND-BOOK

AND

GUIDE TO PIKE'S PEAK,

WITH A

NEW AND RELIABLE MAP,

SHOWING

ALL THE ROUTES, AND THE GOLD REGIONS

OF

WESTERN KANSAS AND NEBRASKA.

ILLUSTRATED WITH APPROPRIATE ENGRAVINGS.

BY PARKER & HUYETT,

Third Street, opposite the new Post Office, and 65 Chesnut Street,

SAINT LOUIS.

1859.

If a strike proved rich enough, a cluster of prospectors' tents and shacks (above) could spawn a prosperous town. Despite its being hailed in print (right), the "strike" at Pike's Peak failed to spawn much of anything.

Despite the Pike's peak debacle, those who wished to search for gold (and silver, as it turned out) still had plenty of reason to go to Colorado. Major strikes occurred at Clear Creek, Idaho Springs, Georgetown, and Silver Plume in 1859. In 1878, a silver rush started near Leadville and spread throughout the state. At Cripple Creek, near Mount Pisgah, a cowboy named Robert Womack stumbled upon gold in 1891. Within five years, twenty-five thousand people lived there, producing $25 million worth of gold. Like so many other mining boomtowns, however, Cripple Creek is now a ghost town.

Meanwhile, in Montana Territory, prospectors found gold at Alder Gulch, Bannack, Virginia City, and Last Chance Gulch (known today as Helena). Ten thousand miners flooded into the area, making the Montana boomtowns some of the wildest in the West. They arrived via the famous trail blazed by John Bozeman, which led them north from the Oregon Trail for 60 miles (97km) along the eastern edge of the Bighorn Mountains and then turned west toward gold country. Prospectors also discovered gold, silver, copper, lead, and other metals in Idaho, Utah, and Arizona.

In Oregon, white prospectors invaded Indian land. They found gold at the mouth of the Clearwater River, which ran through a Nez Percé reservation, in 1860. Twenty thousand sourdoughs rushed to the site by the end of 1862, while the U.S. Army forced the Indians off their land and onto a reservation. In the Black Hills of South Dakota, the army played a different role. After gold was first discovered in 1874, the Sioux who lived in the area threatened to kill any intruders in the sacred hills. The U.S. Army was sent in to keep the prospectors off Indian land, but miners rushed to the area and evaded the blockade. When the troops ejected the illegal mining parties, others took their place. Finally, the army gave up in 1875 and opened the land to anyone willing to risk Indian attack. The miners enjoyed major strikes near Custer City and Deadwood in 1876.

MAKING CONNECTIONS

As the West filled with Americans, the nation found that its great size presented some real problems: Because travel and communication

Subject to Indian attack only rarely, stagecoaches provided the first regular mail and passenger service between the states and the gold fields.

EXPRESS & MAIL ROUTES TO THE WEST, 1858–1875

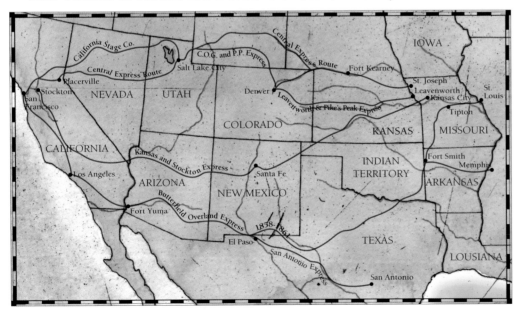

between cities thousands of miles apart were slow and unreliable, it could take weeks for news to travel from one end of the country to the other. The federal government stepped in to forge stronger links between east and west. Beginning in the 1850s, qualified express companies, stagecoach lines, telegraph companies, and railroads received government subsidies to improve transportation and communication across the continent.

In 1858, John G. Butterfield and William G. Fargo launched the nation's first express mail service between the East and the West. The Butterfield Overland Mail offered stagecoach service between Tipton, Missouri, the terminus of eastern rail service, and San Francisco. Two stages per week traveled in each direction, covering the 2,800 miles (4,505km) in twenty-four days. The Butterfield Overland Mail became indispensable as a mail service, but it never attracted many passengers. Each stage could carry nine passengers at a fare of two hundred dollars, but the ride was cramped and jostling. One passenger recounted his experience on the stage by stating, "I know what hell is like. I've had twenty-four days of it."

Starting in the late 1850s, two additional stagecoach lines connected the East and West: the Kansas Stockton Express, which ran from Kansas City to Stockton, California; and the San Antonio Express between San Antonio and San Diego. In 1860, mail service became even faster with the debut of the Pony Express. The freighting firm of Russell, Majors, and Waddell established ten-day mail service between St. Joseph, Missouri, and San Francisco. A total of 190 way stations, built at intervals of 10 miles (16km), served as relay points where mailbags were passed between couriers on horseback. Each rider galloped 70 miles (113km) at a stretch, changing horses at each station. At any given time, eighty riders sped along the trail, forty traveling east and forty west. The ride could be harrowing, as one rider recalled:

> When I arrived at Cold Springs, I found to my horror that the station had been attacked by Indians, and the keeper killed and the horses taken away. What course to pursue I decided in a moment—I would go on. I watered my horse—having ridden him thirty miles [48km] on time, he was pretty tired—and started for Sand Springs, thirty-seven miles away. It was growing dark and my road lay through heavy sagebrush, high enough in some places to conceal a horse. I kept a bright lookout, and closely watched every motion of my poor horse's ears, which is a signal for danger in Indian country. I was prepared for a fight, but the stillness of the night, and the howling of the wolves and coyotes made cold chills run through me at times, but I reached Sand Springs in safety.

Placer mining (top) and hydraulic mining (below) gave wealthy investors access to great reserves of gold and other minerals. The laborers who worked such mines enjoyed uncommon amenities in camp (above).

Most young, white men in the West found prospecting more attractive than regular employment, so Chinese laborers (above) did much of the work on railroads such as the Transcontinental, which was finished with a golden spike (below right).

PRINCIPAL PACIFIC RAILROADS, 1883

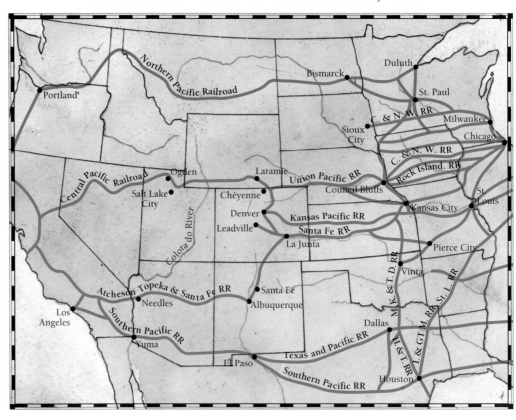

Americans fell in love with the excitement and romance of the Pony Express, but the service proved impractical and unprofitable. In the end, it was put out of business by the telegraph; the first transcontinental line was completed by the Pacific Telegraph Company and the Overland Telegraph Company in 1861.

When California became a state in 1850, entrepreneurs started planning railroad lines to link the two coasts, but the north-south rivalries that sparked the Civil War prevented the federal government from approving any single plan. The outbreak of the war prompted federal officials to designate a northern transcontinental route that ran 1,775 miles (2,856km) between Sacramento, California, and Omaha, Nebraska. Two companies, the Central Pacific and the Union Pacific, received massive grants of land on which to cut timber, quarry stone, and lay tracks. For each mile of rail the companies built, they collected between sixteen thousand and forty-eight thousand dollars The Central Pacific built east from Sacramento and the Union Pacific west from Omaha.

In January 1863, the Central Pacific commenced construction. All its tools and supplies, including locomotives and railcars, had to be shipped to the West Coast by sea, and many of its workers had to be imported from China because of a shortage of cheap labor in California. It took four years for work crews to lay the railroad through the mountains. It took almost as long for the Union Pacific just to get started from the East, as the government did not approve the company's first 40 miles (64km) of track until 1866, and materials and equipment had to be shipped up the Missouri River because there was no railroad connecting Omaha to the East.

Congress declared that each railroad would end wherever the two lines met, precipitating a race between the two companies to build as much line as possible. Traveling by horse and on foot, teams of surveyors preceded the work crews, laying out the course the rails should take. Behind them came the grading crews, who prepared the roadbed with equipment hauled in wagons. Working as fast as they could, they drilled tunnels, filled in depressions, and built bridges. Next came the crews who laid the cottonwood railroad ties, followed by the rail layers, who secured the rails to the ties and moved forward on the newly laid tracks. On average, the railroad advanced 6 to 8 miles (9.7–12.9km) a day. One reporter clocked a team that could lay 240 feet (73m) of rail in 1 minute and 20 seconds.

The main work camp of the Union Pacific, from which construction was supervised, moved west along with the tracks. Known as Hell on Wheels, the tent city had the wild feeling of a gold-rush town. The camp drew adventurers west as it leapfrogged toward the mountains, bringing to the unsettled territories a rough-and-ready sort of society. Frontier settlements sometimes sprang up when the work camps were moved, and some of these settlements ultimately grew into thriving cities like Cheyenne, Wyoming, and Reno, Nevada.

After six years of backbreaking work, the two segments of the transcontinental railroad met at Promontory, Utah. The final spike, made of gold, was driven on May 10, 1869, heralding the completion of the great east-west artery. Even as the nation celebrated, Americans started west by rail. The trip from Nebraska to California now took only four days at a dizzying 30 miles (48km) per hour; soon a bridge over the Mississippi completed the coast-to-coast rail link. Before long, four additional railroads spanned the continent.

The completion of the Transcontinental Railroad and the growth of the rail system throughout the West changed the flavor of pioneer life forever.

CHAPTER 6

THE CATTLE KINGDOM

T

HE COWBOY'S LIFE IS A DREARY LIFE,
THOUGH HIS MIND, IT IS NO LOAD,
AND HE ALWAYS SPENDS HIS MONEY
LIKE HE FOUND IT IN THE ROAD.
—COWBOY SONG

Before the transcontinental railroad shrunk the space between east and west in an instant, most of the continent was populated by indigenous and displaced Indians, U.S. Army troops, and a few white traders. The Great Plains loomed in the American imagination as a stark, desolate barrier between the Mississippi River Valley and the Rocky Mountains. Not until Texas ranchers launched the great cattle drives to Kansas and the northern plains did white Americans settle on the prairie for good.

The cattle drives started in response to the booming American market for beef that arose after the Civil War. The fighting had curtailed the slow but steady trickle of beef to the eastern states from the Southwest, depleting the herds of the upper Mississippi. Both Yankees and Rebels had grown tired of mutton. Meanwhile, huge numbers of European immigrants arrived from across the Atlantic, fueling the rapid growth of the hungry northeastern cities. And the hundreds of thousands of prospectors who filled the mining camps of the western mountains clamored for beef, as did American soldiers posted at forts throughout the plains and mountains.

Texas stood ready to meet the nation's demand for beef. Five million longhorns roamed the state, free for the taking to anyone who could round them up and brand them. With enormous profits to be had, investors and drovers assembled a network of ranches, cattle trails, and stockyards connected to the slaughterhouses of Chicago and St. Louis via the Kansas railheads. In little more than a generation, ten million cattle were driven north along the trails; where the trails met the rails, legendary cattle towns roared for a few short years. As the railroads inched farther west, the era of the long drive came to an end. Ranching spread across the northern plains of Kansas, Nebraska,

Wyoming, Montana, and the Dakotas. Eventually, conflict between farmers and ranchers sparked the "barbed-wire wars" and fenced in the industry.

Along with the rise of the "Cattle Kingdom," there arose the myth of the cowboy. The gun-toting, lasso-wielding, guitar-strumming horseman took his place in the panoply of American heroes. Of course, the realities of life on the range bore little resemblance to fantasies of the Wild West. Frequently Mexican-American, African-American, Native American, or even female, the typical cowboy was more concerned with food, sleep, and the weather than with gunfights, rope tricks, or rustlers. "There is a good deal of exaggeration about us cowboys," one explained. "We're not near so bad as we're painted. We like to get up a little racket now and then, but it's all in play."

TEXAS

First brought to North America in the sixteenth century, cattle arrived in Mexico on the ships of Spanish conquistadores. Gradually spreading north, either driven by ranchers or wandering in wild herds, cattle reached Texas in the eighteenth century. Under the watchful eyes of the Mexican *vaqueros*, the longhorns roamed freely across the range. Americans who migrated to Texas early in the nineteenth century thought the unfenced cattle belonged to no one. So they rounded up the longhorns, branded them, and sold them for their hides, tallow, hooves, and horns. The vaqueros saw these early Anglo cowboys as thieves.

The ensuing tension between Mexican and American ranchers contributed to the outbreak of the Mexican War in 1846. The United States had previously offered to buy Texas, but first Spain and then Mexico (which won its independence from Spain in 1821) refused. Americans streamed into Texas anyway, many to farm cotton in the eastern coastal areas. In 1830, a worried Mexico officially barred further American immigration, but by 1835 about thirty thousand Americans lived in Texas, compared with perhaps three thousand Mexicans. In 1836, the Anglos declared the independence of the Lone Star Republic from Mexico. War

No single image from the American west is such a vivid archetype for the nation's identity as that of the cowboy.

The cattle kingdom was founded in Texas, where Sam Houston (above) led Anglo Americans to independence from Mexico in a war that included the Battle of the Alamo (left).

erupted at the battle for the Alamo, where Davy Crockett and Jim Bowie were killed in a crushing defeat. But within two months, Sam Houston led the Texans to victory.

The Lone Star Republic immediately applied to the United States for statehood, but it was not admitted to the union until 1845. Angered by the annexation of Texas, Mexican soldiers attacked U.S. troops stationed along the Rio Grande. The resulting conflict—which came to be called the Mexican-American War—lasted a year and a half. The United States took California and New Mexico and invaded Mexico, occupying the capital at Mexico City. In the Treaty of Guadalupe Hidalgo, ratified on March 10, 1848, Mexico ceded Texas north of the Rio Grande to the United States. Texas was now indisputably American.

A number of cattle barons built enormous ranches in the twenty-eighth state: John S. Chisum maintained 60,000 to 100,000 head, Charlie Goodnight co-owned the 1.3-million-acre (520,000ha) JA Ranch, Richard King commanded a million and a half acres (600,000ha), and B. H. Campbell boasted the biggest of them all—the XIT Ranch. In Texas before the Civil War, cattle outnumbered people six to one. Still, the ranches of Texas remained isolated from the East, making it difficult to get the beef to market. Initially the market in hides, tallow, hooves, and horns prevailed.

Cattle driving got off to a slow start. One drive took longhorns east to New Orleans and another north to Ohio, while a few herds a year were taken along the Old Spanish Trail from San Antonio to Los Angeles. Before the Mexican War, merchant and cattle trader Oliver Loving had blazed the first of the long northward trails: the Shawnee Trail, which led northeast from Brownsville and Dallas to Kansas City, Sedalia, and St. Louis. Unfortunately, the trail cut through Indian lands, where drovers faced the constant threat of raids, and through areas already settled by white farmers, who sometimes used shotguns to keep the herds away from their crops. Kansas and Missouri made the trail even more problematic when they barred the entry of longhorns during certain seasons because the animals carried ticks that could spread Texas Fever to domesticated livestock. Further adding to the uncertainty of the drive, northern buyers were often skeptical of the tough, scrawny herds that completed the journey. As one St. Louis reporter wrote:

They never ate an ear of corn in their lives. An attempt was made to feed them with corn and provender, but they ran away from it. Texas cattle are about the nearest to wild animals of any now driven to market. We have seen some buffaloes that were more civilized.

Charles Pierce

Charles Goodnight

Richard King

Left: American cattle barons like "Shanghai" Pierce, Charles Goodnight, and Richard King built huge ranches that employed hundreds of cowboys. Above: The men on horseback adopted many time-tested elements of the Mexican vaquero uniform.

Thus, cattle driving remained a limited enterprise until the Civil War, when it stopped altogether. The war put a halt to north-south travel, including cattle driving, thereby confining the longhorns to Texas. Left all but unprotected when the Union called its troops Back East, the ranches suffered frequent Indian attacks. Eighty percent were abandoned during the war, leaving the cattle to roam free again. The wild herds of longhorns grew immense, reaching five million head by the end of the war.

At the same time, railroads now linked Chicago, St. Louis, and Kansas City with locations to the west. When the postwar demand for beef suddenly skyrocketed, ranchers started driving their cattle to these new railheads. Steers that sold for four dollars a head in Texas could be sold for as much as forty dollars a head up north, so anyone who could capture the unbranded mavericks had free access to seemingly unlimited profits. Speculators and dreamers poured into Texas, as well as into Arizona and New Mexico.

The first cattle drives ended in Abilene, where cowpunchers loaded longhorns into freight cars in a maneuver known as a cattle-shoot.

TRAILS

Joining the Anglo, Mexican-American, and Native American cowboys who had long called Texas home, a motley assortment of would-be cattle kings made their way west. Among them were large numbers of criminals fleeing the law, ex-slaves fleeing oppression, and Confederate veterans fleeing Reconstruction. One observer described some of the new cowboys:

> *Here are the drovers, the identical chaps I first saw at Fair Oaks and last saw at Gettysburg. Every one of them unquestionably was in the Rebel army. Some of them have not yet worn out all of their distinctive gray clothing—keen-looking men, full of reserve force, shaggy with hair, undoubtedly terrible in a fight, yet peaceably great at cattle driving and not demonstrative in their style of wearing six-shooters.*

Largely illiterate, the cowboys worked for low wages. Certain specialists, such as the bronc busters or the wranglers, who excelled at roping, might earn a little more, but most cowboys just got by, sleeping in communal bunkhouses, eating whatever food the boss supplied, and wearing anything at hand.

For all cowpunchers, certain items became indispensable. A wide-brimmed hat sheltered the wearer from the elements and a bandanna kept dust out of the mouth. Brown or blue denim pants manufactured by Levi Strauss provided both comfort and protection during long hours in the saddle. The familiar cowboy boots, with their pointed toes and slanted heels, slid in and out of stirrups easily and held the foot in place while riding. Heavy leather chaps shielded the legs while riding through scrub; lined with shearling, they provided warmth in the winter. Each cowboy owned his own saddle, which he prized for its comfort to himself and to his horse. A good set of spurs helped him guide his horse, while a rawhide lariat helped him control the steers. Most cowboys also carried a Colt .44 or .45 six-gun among their possessions, although they seldom wore them.

Cowboys rarely engaged in the quick-draws or shootouts later glamorized by Hollywood. They used their guns for killing predators, putting down crippled livestock, and defending against Indians. This letter from a rancher's wife to her husband describes her use of a gun:

> *Dear Lewis,*
> *The Apaches came. I'm mighty nigh out of buckshot. Please send more.*
> *Your loving wife*

There were plenty of women on the range, and they knew how to handle guns. They also knew how to handle cattle. Some, such as Maude Reed, Susan Haughian, and Sally Skull, were ranchers in their own right with a crew of cowboys working for them. Others were the wives or daughters of ranchers and worked alongside their families. Still others were free spirits who went where they pleased, sometimes passing as men and sometimes joining gangs of rustlers. Whether they wore skirts or trousers, whether they rode astride or sidesaddle, cowgirls often became expert horsewomen and valued members of the outfit. A cowboy song celebrating the ranch woman ran:

> *Miss Agnes rides the gray horse,*
> *Miss Lulu rides the brown;*
> *Young Milton ropes the mavericks,*
> *Miss Agnes ties 'em down.*

A cowboy's work often took him out in the harshest weather to tend his charges (above). Ranch women (below left) performed most of the same tasks as their male colleagues, and were sometimes better at them.

Anglo, Mexican and African-American cowboys worked side by side on many ranches (above).

"Miss Agnes" was Agnes Morley Cleaveland, whose memoir, *No Life for a Lady*, is an account of what it was like to be a cowgirl:

> Although I rode sidesaddle like a lady, the double standard did not exist on the ranch. Up to the point of my actual physical limitations, I worked side by side with the men, receiving the same praise or same censure for like undertakings. I can still hear Bowlegs scoffing at me because a "longear" got away from me in the brush. What kind of brush rider was I that I couldn't keep close enough to a yearling to see where it went?

Brush riding and roping were typical ranch tasks, especially at roundup time. Ranches held two roundups each year. The spring roundup allowed the cowboys to see how the herd had weathered the winter and to determine how many calves had been born. They roped the calves to brand them with the ranch's distinctive symbol and, if they were male, to castrate them so they would fatten into steers. In fall, the roundup prepared the herd for the long drive north. The cowboys branded any roaming mavericks they caught, incorporating them into a herd of several hundred to several thousand head. Keeping track of the brands of different ranches with special notebooks, they separated the herds. Then they set out for the trail.

Texas cattlemen made the first of the long drives along the dangerous Shawnee Trail to Sedalia, Missouri, in 1866. They encountered so many obstacles that only a fraction of the 260,000 head sent out reached market. Most got only partway up the trail before being turned back by Indian resistance. The following year, Joseph G. McCoy temporarily solved the Indian problem by opening a cattle depot in the central Kansas town of Abilene. To reach Abilene, the herds could travel up a much safer trail to the west of the Shawnee. In 1868, ranchers drove 75,000 Texas longhorns to Abilene; by 1871, the number peaked at close to 700,000 head. Over the course of five short years, a total of 1.5 million head passed through Abilene.

The cowboys followed the Chisholm Trail from Texas to Kansas. Originally blazed by Jesse Chisholm, a half-white, half-Cherokee trader, the trail encompassed his trading route and extended beyond it. The operator of several trading posts in the region, Chisholm lived near Wichita. In the fall of 1864, he filled his wagons with goods and set out to trade with the Indians in Indian Territory. He followed the Indian Trail south to Council Grove on the North Canadian River, where Oklahoma City now stands. His route crossed gentle terrain in an area safe from hostile Indians. Chisholm traveled this route regularly and extended it south to the Red River. Other traders and travelers also began using it and took to calling it Chisholm's Trail.

Among the cowpuncher's many chores were roping and branding, which were often performed by specialists.

The Chisholm Trail eventually ran all the way from the Texas-Mexico border in the south to Abilene in the north. Thanks to McCoy's business genius, Abilene became the first of the notorious cattle towns. Texas desperado John Wesley Hardin described the town in its cattle-trading years:

I have seen many fast towns, but Abilene beats them all. The town was filled with sporting men and women, gamblers, cowboys, desperadoes, and the like. It was well supplied with barrooms, hotels, barber shops, and gambling houses; and everything was [always] open.

In 1871, the law-abiding residents of Abilene grew weary of the ruckus made by cowboys at the end of the drive. They decided to evict the cattle industry from their town, drawing up a manifesto to announce their policy:

We the undersigned members of the Farmers' Protective Association and Officers and Citizens of Dickinson County, Kansas, most respectfully request all who have contemplated driving Texas Cattle to Abilene in the coming season to seek some other point for shipment, as the inhabitants of Dickinson will no longer submit to the evils of the trade.

The ranchers knew better than to take their business where it was not wanted. In 1872, cattle drovers took the longhorns up the Chisholm Trail only as far as Wichita, then either sold the cattle there or followed the trail's newly blazed branch to Ellsworth, which lay to the west of Abilene. By 1875, Ellsworth was the terminus for about 1.5 million head per year. Cattle continued to stream up the Chisholm Trail until 1876, when a new trail was opened—leading to Dodge City, Kansas.

On the trail, cowboys ate from the chuckwagon, a specially designed vehicle over which "Cookie" had absolute authority.

Dodge City lay even farther west than Ellsworth, out of the way of the advancing farm frontier. Leading through unsettled country to the west of the Chisholm Trail, the Dodge City Trail led from San Antonio and Austin to Dodge City, then continued to the ranches of North Dakota and Montana. In the years between 1869 and 1884, 7.5 million head of cattle traveled up the trail. Already a notoriously lawless place, Dodge City gained a reputation as the wildest of all the cattle towns. In fact, the arrival of the cattle trade actually took some of the rough edges off the town. Laws were instituted and enforced, and guns were prohibited within city limits. Nonetheless, the cowboys found plenty to entertain them at the end of the drive.

Taking about three months to complete, the long drive isolated the cowboys from all forms of civilization and amusement. To keep discipline among the drovers, many outfits prohibited drinking and gambling on the trail. The rules were enforced by the trail boss and *el secundo*, his right-hand man. Second only to them in authority, the cook reigned supreme around the chuck wagon, a sturdy vehicle equipped with dozens of compartments that held provisions and supplies. Cowboys "rode on their stomachs" and went out of their way to show respect to the cook, who could make or break a drive in his Dutch oven. Only sleep was more important than food on the trail, recalled Teddy Blue Abbot, a well-known cowboy:

I believe the worst hardship we had on the trail was loss of sleep. There was never enough sleep. Our day wouldn't end till about nine o'clock, when we grazed the herd onto the bed ground. And after that every man in the outfit except the boss and horse wrangler and cook would have to stand two hours' night guard. Suppose my guard was twelve to two. I would stake my night horse, unroll my bed, pull off my boots, and crawl in at nine, get about three hours' sleep, and then ride two hours. Then

THE RANCHERS' FRONTIER

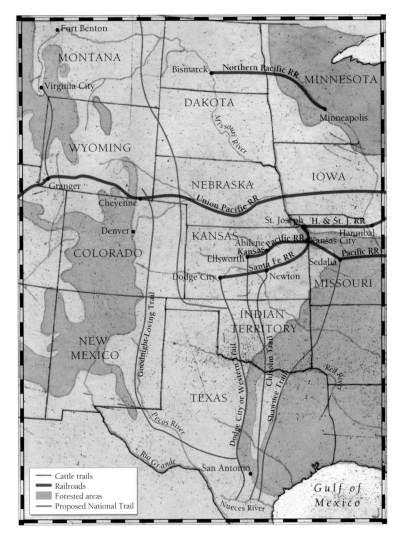

I would come off guard and get to sleep another hour and a half, till the cook yelled, "Roll out," at half past three. So I would get maybe five hours' sleep when the weather was nice and everything smooth and pretty, with cowboys singing under the stars. If it wasn't so nice, you'd be lucky to sleep an hour. But the wagon rolled on in the morning just the same.

Cattle driving was hard work. A team of cowboys spent all day in the saddle controlling a herd of hundreds or thousands of large, wild animals with lethal horns. Each cowboy was responsible for 250 to 300 head and had to help keep the herd moving in the right direction at the

right pace. Cowboys also provided rudimentary veterinary care to the longhorns, hunted down strays and brought them back to the herd, and protected the cattle from Indians, coyotes, rustlers, and rattlesnakes. Most of them rode horses supplied by the company, and each had a *remuda*, a string of six or seven horses for his exclusive use that were kept for him by the horse wrangler. A cowboy rode each of his horses for three hours at a stretch, relying on particular horses to perform specialized tasks, such as night riding.

For the first few days of a drive, the cowboys had an especially difficult time controlling the herd, because cattle would try to return home as long as they were relatively close by. Once the herd got used to the trail, it could advance about 15 miles (24km) a day, grazing as it walked. The drive went on in all kinds of weather; many cowboys riding tall in the saddle were killed by lightning on the open range. Lightning was a big problem at night, when it could spook the cattle and cause a stampede. To soothe the nervous steers in the dark, the two cowboys on night guard often sang quietly. Night watch could be the finest time of the day, according to one cowboy:

To ride around the big steers at night, all lying down as full as a tick, chewing their cuds and blowing, with the moon shining on their horns, was a sight to make a man's eyes pop.

Stampedes were dangerous for cowboys and longhorns alike. Once a herd started stampeding, it would trample over trees, wagons, people, and anything else in its way. A herd might even stampede over a cliff or into a ravine. In 1876, in the worst stampede in history, a huge herd plunged into a gully near the Brazos River, leaving two thousand steers dead or missing. Cowboys stopped stampedes by waving yellow slickers in front of the herd's leaders to direct them into a large circle.

River crossings also ranked among the most hazardous moments on the trail. Cattle could drown in a river with a fierce current or could drown each other by "milling," swimming in a tight circle and pressing in toward its center, forcing cow after cow under the swirling herd. One cowboy recalled how he saved the day at a river crossing in 1871:

I stripped to my underclothes, mounted a big horse called Moore, and went to them. I got off the horse and right onto the

Cowboys driving cattle through Indian territory sometimes encountered "toll collectors" who demanded a side or two of beef as the price for safe passage.

cattle. They were jammed so close together that it was like walking on a raft of logs. When I got to the only real big steer in the bunch on the yon side, I mounted him and he pulled for the shore. When I got near the bank, I fell off and drifted downstream to the horse who had come on across.

The slow, grazing pace of a cattle drive fattened the steers for market. If a drive encountered problems, though, it could leave the cattle exhausted and underweight. Depending on their condition, they would be shipped east by rail or sold to northern ranchers for fattening up.

COW TOWNS

At the end of the trail, cowboys looked forward to a few days of well-earned relaxation and entertainment in the cattle towns. One such town was Caldwell, Kansas, a rail terminus along the Chisholm Trail that the cowboys celebrated in song:

> *We hit Caldwell, and we hit 'er on the fly;*
> *We bedded down the cattle on a hill close by.*
> *You strap on your chaps, your spurs, and your gun,*
> *For you're goin' to town to have a little fun.*

A cowboy finished his three strenuous months on the trail with a hundred dollars in his pocket. The first thing he was likely to do in town was to get a shave, a haircut, and a bath. After that, depending on his tastes, he could head to the saloons, gambling houses, dance halls, or brothels. Often, he would find a "soiled dove" who struck his fancy and would "marry her for a week." Frequently, these women of easy virtue were the only women cowboys knew. A reporter in Newton, Kansas, gave his view of the prostitutes:

> *You may see young girls not over 16 drinking whisky, smoking cigars, cursing and swearing until one almost loses the respect they should have for the weaker sex. I heard one of their townsmen say that he didn't believe there were a dozen virtuous women in town.*

Most infamous among the cattle towns were the Kansas settlements of Newton, Ellsworth, Wichita, Caldwell, Ogallala, and Dodge City. But contrary to popular myth, cowboys seldom shot up the streets in gunfights. True, the cattle towns were wild, but by the time the trails reached these frontier outposts, the rule of law had been established. After the Cattle Kingdom fell, many became quiet, prosperous farm towns.

TROUBLE AHEAD

The long drive was always a risky venture for the ranchers of Texas. All kinds of mishaps could take their toll on herds along the trail, resulting in the loss of many head. As the trails matured, Indians started charging drovers for the right to cross their land. Eventually cattlemen could ship their product north without making the time-consuming trip up the trails. The large Texas ranches continued to prosper, but they soon faced competition from ranches on the northern plains.

In 1866, Charles Goodnight and Oliver Loving blazed the Goodnight-Loving Trail in order to bring cattle directly to the mountain mining camps. The trail curved south and west from the vicinity of Fort Worth to eastern New Mexico Territory, then turned north to Pueblo, Denver, and Cheyenne, avoiding territory inhabited by hostile Indians. The trail not only delivered cattle to market, it also helped bring ranching to the northern plains.

Plenty of free land with good grazing lay within easy reach of the railroads that now branched out across the region. Ranches in the area grew rapidly and became highly profitable. Between 1860 and 1880, the number of head on ranches in Kansas, Nebraska, Wyoming, Montana, and the Dakotas multiplied from about 131,000 to almost 4.5 million. Cattle barons built huge ranches on half a billion acres (200 million ha) of land gained by shady means from Indians, veterans,

Dodge City, Kansas, 1877. 1--Wolf & Co., 2--Smith, Edwards & Co., 3--the old dance hall, 4--wagons loaded with buffalo hides just in from the ranges.

Dodge City, Kansas, was made famous by cowboys restless for fun at the end of the long drive.

Relations between ranchers and settlers were tense, especially when some started putting up barbed-wire fences and others started cutting them down.

homesteaders, and speculators. But the ranchers saw nothing to apologize for. Wyoming cattle king Alexander Hamilton Swan remarked, "In our business we are often compelled to do certain things which, to the inexperienced, seem a little crooked."

For years, cattle wandered freely across the open prairie. The ranchers settled range rights disputes among themselves, for no laws applied. Periodic roundups separated the different herds from one another so the

When a longhorn broke away from the herd, cowboys had to chase it down and rope it before it could start a stampede.

ranchers could keep track of their holdings. With little to do but watch their cattle graze on free grass, the cattlemen of the northern plains got rich. The cowboy earned his keep across the region, watching over the herds in baking summers and frigid winters.

The cattle boom on the northern plains soon resulted in overcrowding and overgrazing on the range. Sheepherders from the West grazed their livestock on the same land, adding to the problem. Rustling became a more serious threat with each passing year. And as a growing numbers of sodbusters carved homesteads out of the prairie, free-ranging cattle trampled crops. A fierce struggle erupted over how the land should be used. One cowboy recalled disdainfully:

> We had all kinds of trouble with the new settlers. They would plow a furrow and if we crossed over they would have us pulled and fined and under no consideration would they allow us to cross unless it was time to bed the cattle and they would give us all kinds of inducements to camp on their land, so they could use the buffalo chips for fuel next winter. They would guard them like a Texas man does a watermelon patch, until they were ripe enough to haul in.

The people of the treeless, stoneless prairie had nothing with which to build fences until Joseph Glidden started selling barbed wire in 1874. Some ranchers also started to fence in huge tracts of land, often as much as 40 square miles (104 sq km). Their illegal fences sometimes stretched across roads; their ranches encompassed fraudulent land claims, government property, and even homesteads already settled by farmers. The farmers fought back by cutting the barbed wire and by petitioning the government, but the cowboys mended the fences and kept their guns handy. Ranchers who wanted to preserve the free range also cut the fences, but they recognized that theirs was a dying way of life. "The trail strangled to death on barbed wire," a descendant of Jesse Chisholm later wrote.

The heyday of the ranchers finally dimmed after a series of disasters in the years 1885 to 1887. The price of beef on the glutted market started to fall in 1885, and the severe winter of 1885–86 destroyed up to 85 percent of the herds, ruining many ranchers. A drought in the summer of 1886 obliterated the grass supply, weakening the remaining cattle. Finally, the winter of 1886–87, possibly the worst winter in American history, claimed close to 50 percent of the dwindling herds. Large corporations and small ranchers alike went out of business, and the Cattle Kingdom fell.

> With my knees in the saddle and my seat in the sky,
> I'll quit punchin' cattle in the sweet by and by.
> Fare you well, old trail boss, I wish you no harm,
> But I'm quittin' this business to go on the farm.
> —Cowboy Song

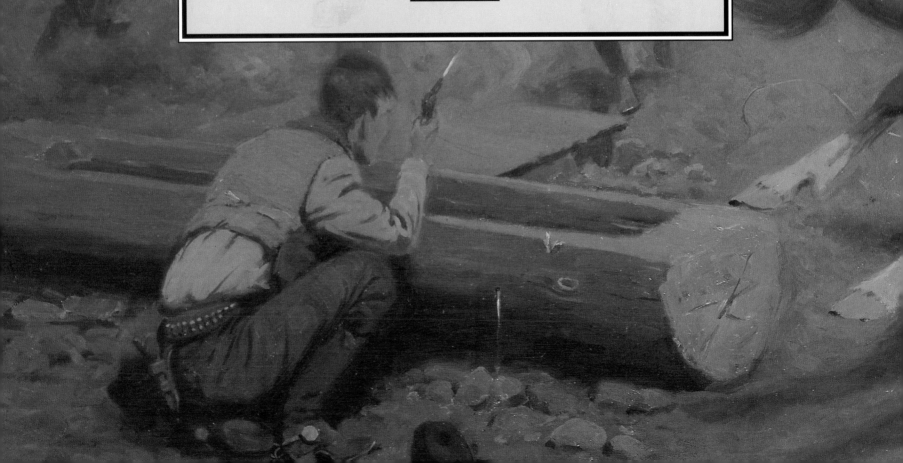

CHAPTER 7

THE WILD WEST

THE ASSORTED PIONEERS WHO TORE INTO THE AMERICAN WEST—TRAPPERS, TRADERS, FARMERS, PROSPECTORS, AND CATTLEMEN—HAD LITTLE IN COMMON WITH ONE ANOTHER BUT A TASTE FOR BONANZA IN ITS VARIOUS FORMS. AMONG THE MYRIAD NEWCOMERS ATTRACTED BY THE FORTUNES TO BE HAD ON THE FRONTIER WERE A PROFUSION OF CRIMINALS. LIKE ANTS TO HONEY, WINDLERS, THIEVES, CONFIDENCE ARTISTS, HOLDUP MEN, CARD SHARPERS, AND OTHER OUTLAWS COULD NOT RESIST THE DRAW OF AMPLE RICHES IN AN OFTEN LAWLESS LAND. FROM CATTLE THAT ROAMED THE OPEN RANGE TO BAGS OF GOLD DUST STACKED IN MINERS' CAMPS TO VALUABLES CARRIED BY STAGECOACH PASSENGERS, MUCH OF THE WEST'S NEW WEALTH SEEMED TO LIE ABOUT CONVENIENTLY UNPROTECTED. IT WAS THE BANDIT'S PROFESSIONAL DUTY TO RELIEVE THE UNWARY OF THEIR EXCESS BELONGINGS. DESPERADOES FLOCKED TO THE FRONTIER IN DROVES FROM THE EASTERN CITIES, FROM THE RUINS OF DIXIE AND EVEN FROM THE BRITISH PENAL COLONY OF AUSTRALIA.

At the same time, few pioneers saw any appeal in a law-enforcement career. The peace officer's lot on the frontier was a difficult one, as most of the isolated communities lacked the proper equipment, training, communications, and other support required. Meanwhile, the people were heavily armed and fiercely independent, with little inclination to do things in any but their own way. And with so much money to be made in the West, the most energetic and ambitious settlers concentrated on improving their own lot. As a result, many of those who served as sheriffs, marshals, judges, and other public officials were at best unscrupulous and self-serving; indeed, many lawmen also had careers as outlaws. In particular, cattle rustlers sometimes joined forces with local farmers and townspeople against the ranchers and got themselves elected to office. A San Francisco newspaper commented on the problem of keeping order on the frontier:

> *There is scarce an officer intrusted with the execution of our*
> *state government, scarce a legislator chosen to frame the*
> *laws...scarce a judicial officer from the bench of the supreme*
> *court down to the clerk of the village justice of the peace, scarce*
> *a functionary belonging to the municipal administration of our*
> *cities and incorporated towns, who has not entered upon his du-*
> *ties and responsibilities as the means of making money...rather*
> *than by any prospective regard to the influence which his official*
> *career may have upon the destinies of the community of which*
> *he has no intention to become permanently concerned.*

Not surprisingly, private citizens frequently found it necessary to take matters into their own hands. Taking form in the mining camps of California and Montana, vigilante justice represented the only means of law enforcement in many western settlements. "Law-abiding" citizens followed an unwritten, ambiguous "code of the West" when deciding who had committed a crime and how he or she should be punished.

The images of the Wild West, as popularized by dime novels and newspaper accounts, among other sources, became fodder for the American imagination well into the twentieth century. One of the most notorious perpetuators of the myth was "Buffalo Bill" Cody, whose Wild West Shows, which featured riding, roping, and other "cowboy" tricks, as well as reenactments of famous battles between Indians and the U.S. Army, brought the West to people all over North America and Europe. In this 1907 reenactment, Indians peacefully go about their business, unaware that they are about to be raided.

Jesse James

Charles Quantrill

Left: One of the original outlaws of the wild west, Jesse "Dingus" James learned his trade from Charles Quantrill, leader of a Civil War guerrilla band. Right: Those with a score to settle against such desperadoes often achieved their goals with a length of rope strung from anything handy—a telegraph pole, perhaps.

This code contained an ever-changing list of precepts, generally including the value of personal honor and the notion that a man's word is his bond. Violations of the code, by such lowlifes as horse thieves, cattle rustlers, road agents, and fence cutters, were met with swift, rough justice. Vigilantes tailored the punishment to the situation except when it came to horse thieves. Because stealing a man's horse could leave him vulnerable in dangerous country, the self-appointed judiciary always gave horse thieves the death penalty. One vigilante described such an execution:

At the mouth of the Musselshell a posse met the marshal and took the prisoners from him. Nearby stood two log cabins close

together. A log was placed between the cabins, the ends resting on the roofs, and the four men were hanged from the log.

WILD LIVES

Despite the efforts of the vigilantes, crime flourished in the American West. One of the original outlaw legends was also one of the most bloodthirsty and, perhaps, the most famous. Jesse James spent sixteen years as an outlaw, robbing banks, stagecoaches, and trains of about $200,000 before his career ended. Born in 1847 and known as Dingus to his friends, he received his criminal training as a Missouri teenager from Charles Quantrill, the "bloodiest man in American history." In

Frank James

Cole Younger

Bob Younger

Left: Frank James, Cole Younger, and Bob Younger formed the ruthless James-Younger gang under the leadership of Frank's famous brother, Jesse. The gang brought terror to the citizens of Missouri in scenes like the one above.

1866, James robbed his first bank with his older brother Frank and the Younger brothers: Cole, Jim, Bob, and John. A Rebel sympathizer, he justified his gang's crimes as retaliation against oppressive Yankees.

The gang viciously bullied the inhabitants of their turf, prompting one newspaper, the *Missouri World*, to report: "So great is the terror that the Jameses and Youngers have instilled in Clay County that their names are never mentioned save in back rooms and then only in a whisper." James was known for his cruelty and for the pleasure he derived from murder. Of one victim he told a friend, "to shoot him down would be too swift. I want him to feel it.... I want to watch him." His brutality finally sealed his doom, when angry citizens of Northfield, Minnesota, surrounded the gang as it robbed a bank. The crowd killed Jim Younger and arrested his brothers, but James escaped to St. Joseph, Missouri. As the gang disintegrated, a friend betrayed him; on April 3, 1882, Bob Ford shot James to death in his hideout.

After their first robbery, the James-Younger gang fled to Texas, where Cole Younger took up with horse thief Belle Starr. Sometimes wearing a velvet gown and sometimes passing as a man, Starr stole the

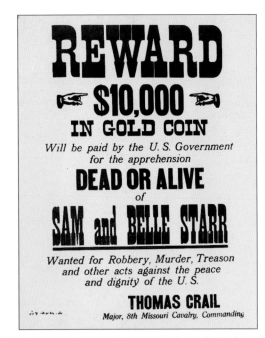

Above: Despite the U.S. government's offer of a huge reward (right), bounty hunters failed to capture horse thief and cattle rustler Belle Starr (left).

iff of Fort Riley, city marshal of Hays City, and marshal of Abilene. Fired from Abilene for shooting a respected saloon keeper as well as his own deputy, he wandered the West aimlessly and appeared briefly in Buffalo Bill's Wild West Show before making his way to Deadwood. There, his luck gave out for good. While Hickok was playing cards on August 2, 1876, Jack McCall shot him in the back of the head for unknown reasons. Hickok died holding the now famous "Deadman's Hand" of aces and eights and was buried nearby in Boot Hill Cemetery.

Among the friends Hickok left behind was Calamity Jane, a fellow Deadwood maverick. Born Martha Jane Canarray in Missouri, she drifted across the West wearing a fringed buckskin coat and trousers, chewing tobacco and drinking whiskey. At various times, she may have worked on the Union Pacific Railroad, on cattle drives, and as a mule skinner, often passing as a man. She gained a colorful reputation in the saloons, which she played up after she met Hickok and went with him to Deadwood. After Hickok's death, she continued to wander, later claiming to have served as a scout under Custer in the Indian wars and to have worked as a prospector, a teamster, an innkeeper, and a rancher. Rumor had her married once or twice and the mother of a

finest horses and took a long string of lovers. In 1869, she became the leader of a gang of cattle rustlers and horse thieves in Indian Territory (Oklahoma), once providing shelter to a hunted Jesse James. She and her Cherokee lover, Sam Starr, were convicted as horse thieves in 1883 and served a short jail term. Returning to her profession after her release, Starr stole many more horses and took many more outlaw lovers before a bushwhacker murdered her in 1889.

Starr and other cattle rustlers operated on the open plains, but many other desperadoes preferred to work the mining camps. Deadwood, in the Black Hills of South Dakota, may have been the wildest of the gold-rush towns; it was so violent that after one holdup, the local newspaper wearily reported, "We have again to repeat the hackneyed phrase, 'the stage has been robbed.'" Outlaws such as California Jack, Bed Rock Tom, and Poker Alice frequented Deadwood, along with Wild Bill Hickok, who hoped to mine his share of gold at the card tables.

Hickok had a reputation as a gunslinger who had killed many men. Before the Civil War, he rode with the Redleg gang in Kansas and drove a stagecoach. He then worked as a scout for the Union Army and for Custer in the Indian wars. During the late 1860s, he served as sher-

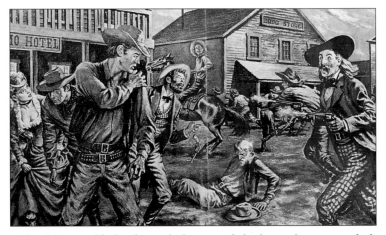

Although it occurred far less frequently than rumored, the shootout became a standard element of western iconography.

Wild Bill Hickok (above left) personified one of the greatest ironies of the Wild West: Many of its lawmen were also notorious criminals, and vice versa. Although not an outlaw, Calamity Jane (above right) ranked among the wildest denizens of the Wild West.

daughter, and in her autobiography she added a stint as Pony Express rider to her résumé. She wrote of one episode from that supposed incarnation:

> I met the overland mail running from Cheyenne to Deadwood. The horses on a run, about two hundred yards from the station; upon looking closely I saw they were pursued by Indians. The horses ran to the barn as was their custom. As the horses stopped I rode along side of the coach and found the driver John Slaughter, lying face downwards in the boot of the stage, he having been shot by the Indians. When the stage got to the station the Indians hid in the bushes. I immediately removed all baggage from the coach except the mail. I then took the driver's seat and with all haste drove to Deadwood, carrying the six passengers and the dead driver.

Late in her life, Calamity Jane occasionally appeared on stage as an authentic artifact of the Wild West. She continued to drink heavily and brawl in bars until she died in 1903 in Deadwood. She was laid to rest in Boot Hill Cemetery beside Hickok.

Where Calamity Jane earned fame with her harmless alcoholic antics, deadly youthful bloodshed brought Billy the Kid into the limelight. Born William Bonney in 1859 in a New York City tenement, the Kid moved to Lincoln County, New Mexico, with his parents. Legend has it that he first killed a man at age twelve for insulting his mother. He fled New Mexico and supposedly killed fourteen more men before returning at age seventeen. Working as a hired gun and rustler during the Lincoln County range rights war, he signed on with any cattleman who paid well and treated him fairly. As leader of a fourteen-man outlaw band, the Kid also kept on killing in numerous skirmishes and shootouts. A Nevada lawman named Pat Garrett finally cornered him

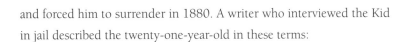

and forced him to surrender in 1880. A writer who interviewed the Kid in jail described the twenty-one-year-old in these terms:

Kid is about 24 years of age, and has a bold yet pleasant countenance. When interviewed between the bars at the jail this morning, he was in a talkative mood, but said that anything he might say would not be believed by the people. He laughed heartily when informed that the papers of [Nevada] Territory had built him up a reputation second only to that of (Apache chief) Victorio. Kid claims never to have had a large number of men with him, and that the few who were with him when captured were employed on a ranch. This is his statement and is given for what it is worth.

Garrett returned the Kid to New Mexico, where he was sentenced to death for the murder of Sheriff William Brady. But the Kid broke out of jail and stayed on the run for seventy-seven days. Garrett and two deputies finally tracked him down at the house of Peter Maxwell on July 14, 1881. There, in Garrett's own words,

We unsaddled here, got some coffee, and, on foot, entered an orchard.... Soon a man arose from the ground, in full view, but too far away to recognize. He wore a broad-brimmed hat, a dark vest and pants, and was in his shirt sleeves. With a few words, which fell like a murmur on our ears, he went to the fence, jumped it, and walked down toward Maxwell's house.... When we reached the porch in front of the building, I left Poe and McKinney at the end of the porch, about twenty feet from the door of Pete's room, and went in. It was near midnight and Pete was in bed. I walked to the head of the bed and sat down on it.... At that moment a man sprang quickly into the door.... The intruder came close to me, leaned both hands on the bed, his right hand almost touching my knee, and asked, in a low tone:—"Who are they Pete?"—at the same instant Maxwell whispered to me. "That's him!" Simultaneously the Kid must have seen, or felt, the presence of a third person at the head of the bed. He raised quickly his pistol, a self cocker, within a foot of my breast. Retreating rapidly across the room he cried:

As a rustler and a killer, Billy the Kid (right) played both sides of the barbed-wire fence in the Lincoln County War. He killed Sheriff William Brady, launching a three-day gunfight. Arrested, tried, and convicted of the sheriff's murder, the Kid then shot his way out of the local jail (above).

Pat Garrett (left) hunted Billy the Kid for seventy-seven days following the Kid's jailbreak, finally shooting him down on July 14, 1881.

Along with his two brothers and aided by Bat Masterson and Doc Holliday, Wyatt Earp brought his own brand of law and order to Dodge City (bottom right). He succeeded against outlaws by adopting some of their methods.

Wyatt Earp

James Earp

Bat Masterson

"Quién es? Quién es?" ("Who's that? Who's that?") All this occurred in a moment. Quickly as possible I drew my revolver and fired, threw my body aside, and fired again. The second shot was useless; the Kid fell dead.

Like Billy the Kid, most gunslingers met an early and violent end. However, this was not true of Wyatt Earp, the buffalo hunter-turned-lawman who never took a bullet and who lived to a ripe old age. He put on his first badge in 1873, at the age of twenty-five. Lounging one day in front of Brennan's Saloon in the cattle town of Ellsworth, Kansas, he watched as an angry crowd gathered to take revenge on Ben Thompson, a customer who had just shot the sheriff. When Earp casually remarked to the mayor that "It's none of my business, but if it was me I'd get me a gun and arrest Ben Thompson or kill him," the mayor handed him the marshal's badge and ordered him into the fray. Earp arrested Thompson, then turned down the marshal's job and headed for Wichita to go into the cattle business.

Preceded by his reputation, Earp was immediately pressed into service as deputy marshal. Two years later, he left a newly peaceful Wichita for the cattle town of Dodge City. Between 1876 and 1879, Earp and his deputies—Bat and Jim Masterson and Joe Mason—tamed Dodge City, with the occasional assistance of a well-armed dentist called Doc Holliday. Accompanied by his brothers Jim, Virgil, and Morgan, and by Holliday, Earp next tackled Tombstone, Arizona. When

Virgil Earp

Doc Holliday

he arrived late in 1879, he was appointed deputy. John Behan, the sheriff, allowed rustlers free rein in the town, a situation Earp was determined to correct. The fight between the deputy's men and the sheriff's men escalated for nearly two years, culminating in the famous shootout at the O.K. Corral. On October 26, 1881, Earp and his men set out to disarm some rustlers, but the confrontation erupted in gunfire. The *Tombstone Epitaph* reported an eyewitness account of the shootout:

> *I was in the O.K. Corral at 2:30 p.m., when I saw the two Clantons (Ike and Bill) and the two McLowrys (Frank and Tom).... I then met Billy Allen and we walked through the O.K. Corral, about fifty yards behind the sheriff. On reaching Fremont street I saw Virgil Earp, Wyatt Earp, Morgan Earp and Doc Holliday, in the center of the street, all armed.... I heard Virgil Earp say, "Give up your arms or throw up your arms." There was some reply made by Frank McLowry, when firing became general, over thirty shots being fired. Tom McLowry fell first, but raised and fired again before he died. Bill Clanton fell next, and raised to fire again when Mr. Fly took his revolver from him. Frank McLowry ran a few rods and fell. Morgan Earp was shot through and fell. Doc Holliday was hit in the left hip but kept on firing. Virgil Earp was hit in the third or fourth fire, in the leg which staggered him but he kept up his effective work. Wyatt Earp stood up and fired in rapid succession, as cool as a cucumber, and was not hit. Doc Holliday was as calm as though at target practice and fired rapidly. After the firing was over, Sheriff Behan went up to Wyatt Earp and said, "I'll have to arrest you." Wyatt replied, "I won't be arrested today. I am right here and am not going away. You have deceived me. You told me these men were disarmed; I went to disarm them."*

Wyatt Earp owed his success to tough talk and a quick gun, but other lawmen of the West relied on a loud gavel and a ready noose. Among the latter was Judge Roy Bean, who brought an iron fist to bear upon Langtry, Texas, a town he named for English beauty Lillie Langtry. Although he never met her, Bean carried a lifelong torch for the actress. That soft spot belied his severity as a judge, which earned him fame as the "Law West of the Pecos." From 1882 to 1902, he dispensed a harsh version of justice, paying little heed to written law. He once acquitted an accused murderer, saying, "it served the deceased right for getting in front of a gun"; another time, he fined a corpse forty dollars for carrying an illegal gun.

If caught, Wild West criminals were often executed. Dispensing with a trial, Wyatt Earp meted out "justice" to Tom and Frank McLowry and Billy Clanton (top, left to right) at the O.K. Corral, while Judge Roy Bean (above, in white beard) dispensed justice and ice-cold beer from the Jersey Lilly, his saloon in Langtry, Texas.

While trying to rob the Condon Bank (above) and another bank in Coffeyville, Kansas, most of the Dalton Boys were killed (right).

Just as austere as Bean, "Hanging Judge" Isaac C. Parker nonetheless let three of the frontier's most notorious brothers slip through his fingers into a life of crime. Briefly employed by the judge, Bob, Grat, and Emmett Dalton soon decided to try the other side of the law. Cousins of the Younger brothers, the Dalton Boys subjected Oklahoma to an eighteen-month reign of terror in 1891 and 1892. In this enterprise, they were joined by seven other bad men, including Bill Doolin. They robbed four trains of sixty-three thousand dollars, then planned a double robbery of the two banks in Coffeyville, Kansas. With Bill Powers and Dick Broadwell, the three brothers rode into town on the morning of October 5, 1892. They split up and entered the two banks simultaneously, then the cry went up in the street: "The bank's being robbed!" Citizens swarmed toward the banks, firing shotguns and revolvers. As they tried to escape, the gang killed four and wounded three townsmen, then were shot themselves. All died but Emmett, who was sentenced to life in prison.

While the fields of bank- and train-robbing were dominated by men like the Dalton Boys, many women outlaws found a niche in cattle rustling. One such woman was Ella "Cattle Kate" Watson, the partner of Jim Averill. Known as "The Duchess of Winchester" for her skill with a rifle, Cattle Kate presided over a Sweetwater, Wyoming, bawdy house owned by Averill. Cowboys traveled miles to visit the only woman in the area, sometimes paying for the privilege with cattle. Averill, meanwhile, rounded up mavericks, applied Kate's brand, and brought them to her corral, angering local ranchers. Even when the savage winter of 1887–88 wiped out many local herds, Kate's herd grew. A posse of vigilantes took its revenge in 1889, lynching Cattle Kate and Jim Averill from a cottonwood tree.

Outlaw women inspired disgust among some Americans and admiration among others. Their exploits became the subject of songs such as this one:

> Hunted by many a posse,
> Always on the run,
> Every man's hand against them,
> They fought, and often won.
> With a price upon each head,
> They'd have to fight and stand,
> And die as game as any man
> With a gun in either hand.

Top: The last of the great Wild West gangs, the Wild Bunch (top) included (standing, left to right) William Carver and Kid Curry, as well as (sitting, left to right) the Sundance Kid, the Tall Texan, and Butch Cassidy. Above: Another member, Black Jack Ketchum, was hanged on April 24, 1901.

North of Cattle Kate's haunts, other rustlers gathered at a Wyoming hideout known as Hole in the Wall. The name referred to a deep gorge that served as the only entrance to a desolate valley populated by all kinds of desperadoes. Large numbers of criminals congregated there in the 1880s, traveling down the outlaw trail as far as Robber's Roost in southeastern Utah to conduct business. Among them were some of the better-known members of the Wild Bunch, such as Black Jack Ketchum, Robert LeRoy Parker (alias Butch Cassidy), Della Rose, and Etta Place.

Larger and better organized than any previous Wild West gang, the Wild Bunch was the last of the region's noteworthy and nefarious mobs. Late in the 1890s, Cassidy and his right-hand man, Harvey "Kid Curry" Logan, as well as Harry Longbaugh, known as the Sundance Kid, led the gang. Based at Hole in the Wall, they ventured out to rob banks, trains, stagecoaches, and even entire towns, shooting and killing along the way.

An outlaw since his teens, Butch Cassidy was born in 1866, the first of thirteen children. He rustled cattle around Robber's Roost, then robbed banks and trains with the McCarty gang of Colorado. On the lam from 1890 to 1894, he worked as a cowhand and as a butcher in Wyoming, then he stole some horses and served two years in prison. Cassidy returned to Hole in the Wall as soon as he was released. In 1897, he held up a mining camp in Utah and announced the formation of the Train Robbers' Syndicate; he was now the leader of the Wild Bunch. A series of flashy train robberies ensued, the last in 1901. By that time, agents of Pinkerton's National Detective Agency were hot on their heels, and the gang split up. Cassidy, the Sundance Kid, and Etta Place headed south of the border as the days of the Wild West drew to a close.

WILD IMAGINATIONS

No one did more to popularize the Wild West phenomenon than William F. "Buffalo Bill" Cody. A hunter and scout, he first came to public attention in 1869, as the subject of Ned Buntline's dime novels. These novels, which greatly exaggerated Buffalo Bill's exploits, made him an icon of the Wild West. In 1883, capitalizing on his notoriety, he started producing a cowboy act called Buffalo Bill's Wild West Show.

The show featured fancy riding, rope tricks, and other "cowboy action," including dramatic sketches concerning cowboys and Indians. Largely fanciful, the show ran for thirty years, firmly establishing a glamorized image of cowboys, cowgirls, and the Wild West in the American psyche. The show spawned many imitators, such as Pawnee Bill's Historical Wild West Show, which promised customers a glimpse of "beauteous, dashing, daring and laughing Western girls who ride better than any other women in the world."

Alongside the male performers, a dozen women also starred in Buffalo Bill's show by 1887, executing feats of trick riding, sharpshooting, and bronc riding. The most famous of all was Annie Oakley. Born Phoebe Ann Moses, she learned to handle guns at an early age and became an expert shot. She married renowned marksman Frank Butler after beating him in a shooting match, then joined Buffalo Bill's show in 1885. Oakley was not an actual cowgirl, but she was a peerless shot, inspiring Sioux chief Sitting Bull to nickname her "Little Sure Shot." In 1893, when the Wild West Show toured Europe, she is said to have shot the ashes off a cigarette in Kaiser Wilhelm's mouth.

The Wild West that survives in the American imagination is part fact and part invention, far more colorful and rollicking than the real thing ever was. Perhaps the threads of truth and fiction that run through the stories of the outlaws will never be separated. But, reality or fantasy, the Wild West has left an indelible mark on American culture against which all manner of danger and adventure is measured.

Buffalo Bill Cody (top right) traversed the dying frontier to recruit talent for his Wild West show (left). Among his stars was Annie Oakley (top left), who learned to shoot after her father died when she was five years old and she assumed responsibility for hunting for the family's food.

CHAPTER 8

ONE HUNDRED
SIXTY ACRES

Y OU MAY STAND ANKLE DEEP IN THE SHORT GRASS OF THE UNINHABITED WILDERNESS; NEXT MONTH A MIXED TRAIN WILL GLIDE OVER THE WASTE AND STOP AT SOME POINT WHERE THE RAILROAD HAS DECIDED TO LOCATE A TOWN. MEN, WOMEN AND CHILDREN WILL JUMP OUT OF THE CARS, AND THEIR CHATTELS WILL TUMBLE OUT AFTER THEM. FROM THAT MOMENT THE BUILDING BEGINS.

—*EYEWITNESS TO THE LAND RUSH*

The Great Plains was the last region of the United States to be settled by whites. Almost featureless except for a few canyons, buttes, and hills, treeless but for clumps of cottonwood along the creeks and riverbanks, the flat and sparsely populated grassland stretched from the Rio Grande in the south almost to the Great Lakes in the north and from the Mississippi River in the east to the Rocky Mountains in the west. Enormous herds of bison grazed there. White Americans had long considered the plains the "Great American Desert" that stood between the continent's burgeoning coasts. But as the nation flourished, growing numbers of settlers came and carved farms out of the tough sod. After 1842, the federal government encouraged further immigration through the Pre-Emption Law, which granted established plains farmers and new settlers the right to buy a quarter section of 160 acres (64ha) for $1.25 per acre. Thanks to this compelling incentive, more homesteads soon appeared on the plains.

FREE LAND (SORT OF)

Public interest in the potential of the plains grew slowly but steadily in the 1840s and through the 1850s. At the same time, the federal government sought ways to strengthen the links between the eastern states and the territories of the West. It soon became clear that settlement of the plains by whites would serve the interests of both the federal government and the American people. To encourage settlers to head west, Congress passed the Homestead Act, which President Abraham Lincoln signed into law in 1862. Under its provisions, any citizen or immigrant with the proper papers, who was either over twenty-one or the head of a family, could claim 160 acres (64ha) of publicly held land for only ten dollars. After five years of residence and the payment of a few more fees, the claimant could gain final title to the tract, as long as he or she made a few basic improvements, such as the addition of fences, barns, and house. To prevent fraud, homesteaders were required to swear that the land was for their own use when they filed a claim.

Government Land Office agents, each of whom had responsibility for a district of 20,000 square miles (51,800 sq km), found it impossible to enforce the law's requirements. Land speculators moved in to take advantage of the situation, perpetrating various kinds of highly profitable fraud. Since the Homestead Act applied only to land that the government had surveyed, some speculators who kept a step ahead of the surveyors could use the Pre-Emption Act to buy up choice, unsurveyed land. To acquire desirable blocks of surveyed land, they hired drifters to put in claims under the Homestead Act and live on them for a few months before signing them over.

Speculators also gained from the Morrill Land-Grant Act of 1862, which assigned extensive acreage to states in order to promote agricultural education. The states did set up the so-called land-grant universities, but they also enriched their treasuries by selling giant parcels to speculators at fifty cents per acre. When it became apparent that 160 acres of arid prairie could not support a family, Congress passed the Timber Culture Act of 1873, which granted homesteaders another 160 acres if they planted 40 of those acres with trees within four years. Again, speculators abused the law, securing some of the best land on the plains and selling it to farmers at five to ten dollars per acre.

When they first arrived on the prairie, many pioneer families built homes by digging into hillsides and constructing walls of sod.

Legitimate corporations also set ethics aside to profit from the government's huge real estate giveaway. To foster the construction of railroads throughout the prairies, the government granted them right-of-way zones where they could select the best course for their new spurs. These long strips of land were 20 to 80 miles (32–128km) wide and were split into ten to forty sections per mile. Railroad-owned acreage alternated with free acreage in a staggered pattern on either side of the tracks. Especially valuable for its proximity to transportation, much of this land ended up in the hands of speculators. The railroads also sold some of their land directly to settlers at high rates. Those who could not afford this land were forced to settle miles away from the rail lines.

The Desert Land Act of 1877 allowed ranchers, who required spreads of 2,000 to 50,000 acres (800–20,000ha), to gain control of a great deal of western land. The act parceled out claims of 640 acres (256ha) to be improved by irrigation. Cattlemen sidestepped the irrigation requirements and paid their ranch hands to put in claims for adjacent land, which were then transferred to the cattlemen. Lumber companies perpetrated the same type of fraud under the Timber and Stone Act of 1878. In addition, the federal government sold some land directly to speculators and permitted Indians to do so as well.

In all, about half a billion of the finest acres (200 million ha) of Great Plains real estate were snapped up by speculators and businessmen, while only 600,000 patents totaling 80 million acres (32 million ha) went directly to homesteaders. Farmers and others who wished to settle on the prairie thus had too often to choose between poor but free land and good but expensive land. However, the persevering and re-

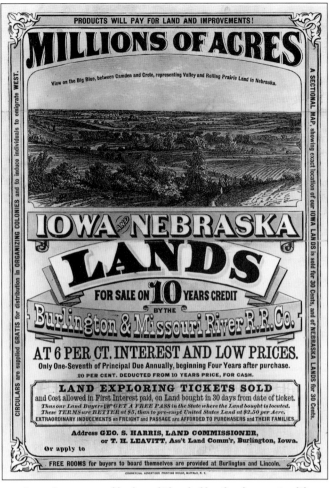

Granted vast tracts of land on which to build, railroad companies did everything they could to lure settlers to travel west by rail and buy company-owned real estate.

sourceful homesteaders learned how to manipulate the claim system themselves and managed to build thriving farms. Some bought out the claims of their neighbors, others sent all offspring who could pass for twenty-one to register claims to adjacent land. Determined to own a farm and make it prosper, about two-thirds of all sodbusters made good on their claims.

STAKING A CLAIM

The Civil War temporarily detained most homesteaders, but when peace broke out a torrent of farmers, veterans, and former slaves headed for the plains. Most of the white American settlers came from the overcrowded states along the Mississippi River and from depleted farms in the Old Northwest (Indiana, Ohio, Illinois, Michigan, and Minnesota). A sizable number of foreign immigrants, mostly from Canada, Ireland, Germany, and the countries of Scandinavia, also came to the plains. For the most part, the "sod-busters," as they came to be called, had agricultural experience, plus enough money to move and to buy the necessary equipment and supplies. But some, drawn by a strong desire to make a fresh start on their own land, arrived with little more than the clothes on their back.

Among these were the African-American "Exodusters," former slaves who hoped to escape white brutality and discrimination in the Reconstruction South. The first organized group of Exodusters arrived in Kansas with Henry Adams of Louisiana, an ex-slave who organized the "Exodus of 1879." Inspired by their example, twenty thousand to forty thousand African-Americans moved to Kansas in the land rush years, claiming perhaps 20,000 acres (8,000ha) of land. Others migrated to Oklahoma under the leadership of another Exoduster, Edward

A sizable contingent of African-American settlers moved west during the land rush, founding towns such as Red Bird, Oklahoma (far right). E.P. McCabe (right), a leading Oklahoma politician, promoted black settlement and education in the territory.

P. McCabe. These farmers joined hundreds of African-American cowboys and "Buffalo Soldiers" in establishing a vital African-American presence on the frontier.

Eager to attract settlers, the plains territories and states touted their virtues in advertisements published not only in the East but also across the Atlantic. Steamship companies and railroads also publicized the bounty of the West in the United States and Europe, hoping to attract passengers and to establish a lasting demand for freight and passenger service along their new spurs. Their pitches made the prairies out to be the land of milk and honey: in a pamphlet issued by Union Pacific, Dakota was described as a paradise where "mocking birds and gorgeous paroquets and cockatoos warble musical challenges to each other amid the rich foliage of the sweet-bay and mango trees," while the Burlington rail line claimed that "many fields of properly cultivated wheat have yielded over thirty bushels of grain per acre, and many fields of corn over seventy."

In the last three decades of the nineteenth century, this kind of propaganda lured millions of settlers to the plains. Many arrived with unrealistically high expectations of their new home, ignorant of the formidable obstacles they faced. In reality, it took two or three years to establish a self-supporting farm on the prairie, and some newcomers were unwilling to endure the intervening hardships. Fred Martin, a pioneer in North Dakota, reflected on the difficulties of staking a claim with his wife, Sophie:

Often nothing made sense to me, and it was a good thing that I had no time to think about Sophie's reproaches. We were stuck on this prairie and had to endure it and hope it would be kind enough to produce food.... We were so lacking in tools and items for changing the rugged prairies into productive farm land that when I think back to our first year on that coyote land, I can hardly keep from crying.

One of the first hurdles the homesteader encountered when establishing a claim was the wrath of cattlemen. Ranchers had grown accustomed to grazing their steers on mile after mile of unfenced grassland, and to driving their herds to market over open range. The farmers, however, needed to protect their crops from the trampling hooves of the longhorns. They fenced their land with barbed wire, and conflict between the two groups often became ugly, as frontier writer Mari Sandoz recalled:

The thin crust of security we thus built over our existence was rudely and finally broken by a horseman who rode wildly into our yard, his rifle balanced across his saddle. He had fenced a little Government land near a large ranch, and that morning he found an old whiskey bottle on his doorstep. In it was a rifle shell wrapped in an unsigned note telling him to get out or be carried out.

But neither ranchers' threats nor speculators' exploitation could chase the sodbusters from their farms. They had dreams to pursue and challenges to meet.

BEATING THE ODDS

Once they registered their claims, homesteaders set about building homes. Some families spent their first months or even years living in an abandoned railroad boxcar or in a dugout shelter. Dug into a sloping riverbank or hillside, dugouts featured a front wall and roof of sod. Cramped and dirty, they also had the drawback of a hillside roof accessible to livestock. Cows or horses that wandered onto a dugout roof to graze sometimes crashed through to the living space below, to the dismay of one and all.

At some point in their frontier career, 90 percent of prairie pioneers lived in a sod house. The homesteaders built houses of sod bricks because there were no trees or timber on the plains. One observer described the construction and quality of the sod house, or "soddie," as it was known:

Sod bricks were made by turning over furrows on about half an acre of ground where the sod was thickest and strongest. Care was taken to make the furrows of even width and depth.... For the first layer of the wall the three-foot bricks were placed side by side around the foundation except where the door was to be made. The cracks were then filled with dirt and two more layers

were placed on these.... A door frame and two window frames were set in the wall and the sod built around them at the proper time...the gables were built up of sod or frame according to the means of the settler.... The little sod cabin was frequently divided into two rooms by a piece of rag carpet or quilt. The windows and door were closed with buffalo robes or other blankets.... The dirt and straw kept dropping on everything.... The most disagreeable feature of these houses was the leaky roof...after a heavy rain it was necessary to hang all the bed clothing and wearing apparel on the line to dry.... [But] it was cool in summer and warm in winter. There was no fear of the wind blowing it over and no danger of destruction by prairie fires.

Above: They may have lived in sod houses, but ambitious pioneer families imported all the comforts of home from Back East. Below: As the homesteaders established thriving farms, they abandoned their first crude shelters for finer sod dwellings.

The soddie presented a number of inconveniences to the frontier homemaker. With only two windows made of greased paper or parchment, the house was dark and stuffy. The dirt floor and leaking roof made it impossible to keep clean, while a heavy rain could cave in the roof. But most soddies lasted around seven years, and some sodbusters built entire settlements, called "dobey towns," out of sod.

The lack of trees on the prairie made finding fuel for fires especially difficult. Homesteaders discovered they could burn buffalo or cow chips, but as hunters wiped out the buffalo herds, the chips grew scarce. Eventually, the railroads brought coal to the western settlers. Whatever they used as fuel, the pioneers knew to be very careful with fire. The tiniest stray spark could ignite the dry prairie grass in an instant, starting a fire that would rapidly rage out of control. A prairie fire could burn for days, consuming mile after mile of grass. The settlers learned how to protect their homes by plowing firebreaks, by burning off the grass around their house and by setting backfires.

In addition to fire, the homesteaders encountered natural disasters such as hailstorms that pounded crops to the earth, tornadoes that leveled homes and towns, droughts that parched the soil, and springtime floods caused by melting snow. Insects constantly preyed on crops, and occasionally great swarms would mow down all plant life in their paths. The worst insect plague struck in the summer of 1874, when mile-wide clouds of grasshoppers swept over the plains from Dakota to Texas. Sometimes covering the fields in a seething, knee-deep blanket, the grasshoppers ate everything from crops and hay to wooden tools and fence posts. In the wake of the ruination, hundreds of homesteaders threw in the towel and returned east, their wagons hung with placards that read, "From Kansas, Where It Rains Grasshoppers, Fire, and Destruction."

Year-round, the sodbusters withstood ceaseless, arid winds. Merciless sun and 110°F (43°C) weather baked the treeless, shadeless prairie in summer, while in winter the temperature plunged to 20 or 30 degrees below zero (-29–-34°C). Animals forced to stay outdoors were covered with thick coats of ice; others were brought indoors to live alongside families. When the ferocious prairie blizzards started, snow would blow through every chink and crack in a house, covering floors, furniture, and everything else with several inches of snow. The complete lack of visibility in the storm posed the terrible risk of getting lost

With wood scarce and coal expensive, prairie settlers turned to cow and buffalo chips for fuel (top). The steady stream of newcomers arriving by rail spurred the growth of towns along railroad routes (above).

and freezing to death, so settlers strung ropes between houses and outbuildings to find their way around. And when the sun finally came out again, the endless white glare of the snow could blind an unwary farmer. Wading through hip-deep drifts to rescue stranded livestock after a blizzard, Mari Sandoz went snow-blind as a teenager. She remembered what happened when she returned home from her day's labors:

"Why don't you light the lamp?" I demanded.

Mother made a funny gurgling noise. "Ah-h," her voice choked. "The lamp is lit. You are blind!"

Before morning I was delirious with pain and sunburn fever. Scorching pinwheels whirled in my head. Father gave me a small dose of morphine to quiet my screams, and when that wore off, another. But he dared not give me any more. My eyes burned like seething, bubbling lead. My head seemed tremendously large, bursting.... The slightest infiltration of light under my bandage maddened me with pain. And when I finally took my bandage off, I found I could aim a gun without closing my left eye. It was blind.

Pioneers on the Great Plains built "cyclone cellars" (above) for protection during tornadoes, and plowed "firebreaks" (below) to prevent prairie fires from burning out of control.

Sodbusters not only engaged in frequent battles with the elements but also fought daily battles to provide for themselves. Work on a homestead was endless and exhausting for men and women alike. Women made their own soap from ashes and animal grease, improvised candles of fat, extracted laundry starch from potatoes, crafted brooms from cornstalks, and turned flour sacks into clothing, curtains, towels, handkerchiefs, and anything else that came to mind. If they lived near a creek, they carried water home by hand or in wagons; if they didn't, they collected rainwater in barrels. The water supply was both meager and dangerous: those who drank it frequently came down with "prairie fever"—typhoid.

To feed their family, women kept a vegetable garden and some fruit trees, preserving the produce in jars for the winter. The daily diet also included salt pork, bacon, beans, corn, cornbread, hominy grits, game, and sometimes a few canned goods. Women prepared everything from scratch, using ingredients close at hand. These self-sufficient pioneer wives might go months at a time without seeing another woman. In combination with the constant drudgery, the enforced isolation of women stranded in their homes on the prairie resulted in profound loneliness, crushing depression, and strained marriages. Pauline Diede, who grew up on a homestead in North Dakota, deplored the lot of her mother and of other women homesteaders:

Pioneer mothers, like my own, journeyed through life meeting hardships and denials, many dying of a broken heart for want of a word of praise, and few knowing how much they left behind.... Not only did she look after her household and the hundreds of duties there, she was expected to be first hand help with outdoor work. Her day began at dawn and did not end until the small hours. The family's livelihood often demanded of a woman

something beyond human endurance. Cooking and sewing for large families turned women into old ladies before their time.

Pioneer men also fought a daily battle for survival. To water their crops, they had to dig wells deep into the earth and build windmills to pump the water out. Eventually, mechanized drilling became available, but it was very expensive. Yet because prairie streams were so small and sluggish, they could rarely be used for irrigation. Most sodbusters turned to a new method of cultivation, known as dry farming. The technique called for deep furrows that could bring subsurface water to the roots of the crops. Soon after a rainfall, dry farmers harrowed the soil in their fields to turn the wet top layer under and prevent evaporation. They also tried new crops better suited to the prairie environment and soon found they could grow hard wheat of very high quality.

Homesteaders plowed their fields with steel shares pulled by teams of oxen or mules, walking behind the plows to guide them. Where the sod was particularly tough, they might need to harness up to three teams to the plow at once. Slowly, the labor-intensive demands of prairie farming led to the invention of various mechanized farming implements. Manufacturers introduced plows with a seat for the farmer and multiple shares to cut more than one furrow at a time. All kinds of planting machines came on the market, as did mowing machines and hay loaders. Mechanical reapers and binders could cut and bind bundles of grain, threshing machines could separate the kernels, and special milling equipment could process hard wheat. Originally powered by horses or other draft animals, some of these devices later switched to steam power.

HERE TO STAY

As the sodbusters learned how to cultivate crops on the prairie, the production rates of their farms exceeded those of eastern farms.

Subject to unending chores and brutal isolation, pioneer women quickly learned to combine work with a social life. The cooperative spirit contributed greatly to the survival of prairie farms and towns.

White settlers brought the great American pastime to the West. Records state that this 1880s baseball game between the towns of Guthrie and Oklahoma City ended in a tie and the re-match ended in a riot.

Investors saw the potential of large-scale farms, which could yield up to 25 bushels (881L) of grain per acre at profits of 100 percent or more. Purchasing tracts of 5,000 to 100,000 acres (2,400–40,000ha), these entrepreneurs hired large crews of laborers and equipped their farms with the most advanced machinery. Thus were born the Dakota "bonanza farms" of the 1870s.

The influx of families (as opposed to single men) to the plains rapidly expanded the region's population and brought large numbers of women to the frontier. Settlers pushed across the prairies along the routes of railroads and the courses of rivers. As more people arrived and farmers enjoyed success, small towns and even cities of several thousand flourished. The sodbusters now had neighbors with whom to share the trials and rewards of homesteading. A tradition of mutual assistance arose, joining neighbors in barnraisings and quilting bees. Those who lived far from railroads combined their resources and brought crops to market in trains of wagons pulled by as many as ten teams of oxen. The settlers also enjoyed relaxing together, often gathering for dances, foot- and horse-races, baking and plowing contests, and ball games. Cooperative work and play alike provided a welcome respite from the isolation of the prairie.

For the most part, Indians posed little threat to the early sodbusters. They occasionally approached white farms to beg or to steal horses, but whites and Indians usually kept their distance from each other. As the number of settlers on the plains swelled, however, conflicts between the two groups became more frequent. Fear of Indian attack haunted every pioneer on the plains, for the encounters, when they happened, could be grisly. Lavina Eastlick, wife and mother of five young sons, survived an attack (with one of her children) during the August 1862 Sioux revolt, known as the bloodiest massacre in the history of the West. Warned of the approach of Indian warriors, the Eastlicks and about thirty others gathered at a neighbor's large log house. The Indians forced them out into the open and a gunfight ensued, in which Mrs. Eastlick's husband and two of her children were killed. She was shot in the foot, head, and back. She later described what happened next:

> I tried to move and found I could crawl. I had gone a few yards out of the trail when a young Indian came along and pounded me over the head and shoulders with a rifle. I expected every moment he would take my scalp, but he did not. He threw the rifle down by my side and went on. I remained perfectly still.... I could not find my children. I imagined they had gone to sleep somewhere among the dead and wounded. About nine or ten o'clock [the next morning] the Indians came back to where

Pioneer farmers learned to conquer the elements with mechanized combines and other technology (right), but they had a harder time with the Indians they displaced. Desperate Native Americans sometimes resorted to violence, as at the Sioux massacre in Big Stone Lake, Minnesota (below left), and in scalpings in Mormon country (below right) and elsewhere.

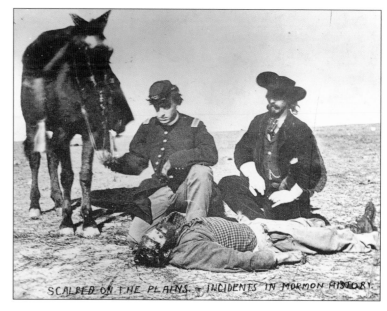

SCALPED ON THE PLAINS. — INCIDENTS IN MORMON HISTORY.

they had fought our folks. I heard them shooting. During the day I heard the children crying most of the time; sometimes I heard them screaming and crying. I could not see them, for I had gone over the ridge a little. No one can imagine my feelings. I wished I could die. I thought then, and think now, that they were torturing the children. It was a great punishment to me to hear the children crying and moaning under the cruel tortures of the Indians. I thought they were my children that I heard. I wanted to die, and yet I feared to die by the hands of the Indians. Had I not feared this horrible mode of death, I should have run away out of hearing of these innocent sufferers. About four o'clock in the afternoon I heard three guns fired. The children then ceased crying.

Despite the risks, a special breed of white settlers known as "Boomers" pushed into the fertile, unoccupied areas of Indian Territory in the 1880s. The railroads clamored to build there, but the federal government resisted pressure to open the land. Although U.S. troops were sent to keep the Boomers out of the area, many slipped in anyway. When the soldiers found and ejected them, they simply returned and set up camp again. In 1883, forty thousand Boomers formed a group called the Oklahoma Colony to initiate organized resistance to the government's blockade. Declaring they would fight for the land, several bands of squatters entered Indian Territory and were once again ejected. But public sentiment in favor of white settlement in Indian Territory mounted, and in 1885 the government voided all Indian claims to unoccupied zones in the territory.

As whites moved in, the government forced displaced Creek and Seminole groups to sell their land to the United States in March 1889. When the announcement went out that this land would open to whites at noon on April 22, 100,000 so-called "Sooners" crowded to the perimeter of the area. When the appointed hour struck, they rushed across the plains on horseback, in buggies, and in wagons. Within a few hours, nearly 2 million acres (800,000ha) had been claimed. Thousands of tents formed the towns of Guthrie and Oklahoma City; a year later, Congress officially designated the area the Oklahoma Territory.

In the years that followed, a series of government actions opened other sections of Indian Territory to white settlement. When the 6 million acres (2.4 million ha) of the Cherokee Outlet were released in 1893, 100,000 Boomers repeated the mad rush of four years earlier.

Left: Sooners raced to stake claims on newly opened land in Oklahoma Territory, where the U.S. government steadily carved away at Indian lands. Right: The government's real-estate giveaway in Oklahoma created instant towns where settlers waited for land and staked their claims.

Starting with nothing but land, homesteaders established a permanent white presence on the Great Plains, the last American frontier.

More and more land opened to white settlement, until the territory gained the final shape of the state of Oklahoma. In the end, the prairies were completely settled by whites.

Perhaps more than any other episode of white incursion into the American West, the settlement of the plains, and their transformation into farmland by the sodbusters, carries the most lasting significance. Writer Wallace Stegner, who grew up on prairie homestead, expressed this notion when he wrote:

Only one who has lived the dream, the temporary fulfillment, and the disappointment [of the frontier] has had the full course.

He may lack a thousand things that the rest of the world takes for granted...but he will know one thing about what it means to be an American, because he has known the raw continent, and not as a tourist but as a denizen. Some of the beauty, the innocence, and the callousness must stick to him, and some of the regret.... Anyone who has lived on a frontier knows the inescapable ambivalence of the old-fashioned American conscience, for he has first renewed himself in Eden and then set about converting it into the lamentable modern world. And that is true even if the Eden is, as mine was, almost unmitigated discomfort and deprivation.

CHAPTER 9

WARRIORS AND REFUGEES

IN ANCIENT TIMES IT WAS PROPHESIED BY OUR FOREFATHERS THAT THIS LAND WOULD BE OCCUPIED BY THE INDIAN PEOPLE AND THEN FROM SOMEWHERE A WHITE MAN WOULD COME. HE WILL COME EITHER WITH A STRONG FAITH AND RIGHTEOUS RELIGION WHICH THE GREAT SPIRIT HAS ALSO GIVEN TO HIM, OR HE WILL COME AFTER HE HAS ABANDONED THAT GREAT LIFE PLAN AND FALLEN TO A FAITH OF HIS OWN PERSONAL IDEAS WHICH HE INVENTED BEFORE COMING HERE. IT WAS KNOWN THAT THE WHITE MAN IS AN INTELLIGENT PERSON, AN INVENTOR OF MANY WORDS, A MAN WHO KNOWS HOW TO INFLUENCE PEOPLE BECAUSE OF HIS SWEET WAY OF TALKING AND THAT HE WILL USE MANY OF THESE THINGS UPON US WHEN HE COMES.... WE KNEW THAT THE WHITE MAN WILL SEARCH FOR THE THINGS THAT LOOK GOOD TO HIM, AND THAT HE WILL USE MANY GOOD IDEAS TO OBTAIN HIS HEART'S DESIRE, AND WE KNEW THAT IF HE HAD STRAYED FROM THE GREAT SPIRIT HE WOULD USE ANY MEANS TO GET WHAT HE WANTS. THESE THINGS WE WERE WARNED TO WATCH.

— HOPI PROPHECY

As whites moved into the American West, they pushed its indigenous peoples out of their ancestral homelands. Certain that they were fulfilling the Manifest Destiny of the United States by occupying the continent from coast to coast, the overwhelming majority of whites saw nothing wrong with killing Indians or confining them to reservations. The pioneers most often saw Native Americans as "savages" who did not know how to work the land as God intended it to be worked. White trappers overhunted the land and exterminated game; homesteaders destroyed hunting grounds and kept Indians off their farms; cattlemen drove huge herds through buffalo country, overgrazing the range and disrupting ancient migration patterns.

The federal government first attempted to protect the Indians by prohibiting whites from selling liquor to them and by designating funds for their "civilization" and education in white ways. But experience soon showed that the restless white settlers and the independent Indians could not live together in harmony. Before long, Congress institutionalized the pioneers' informal pattern of forcible Indian eviction.

During the first half of the nineteenth century, responsibility for Indian relations fell to the War Department. The department set up trading "factories" in Indian country, where government agents encouraged Indians to accumulate debt. When a tribe's bill grew large enough, the agents would persuade them to pay it off by ceding land. Chiefs often sold land without the agreement of other chiefs whose people also lived there; U.S. troops would then arrive to evict the reluctant Indians from land they still believed was theirs. Chief Joseph of the Nez Percé used an analogy to characterize the practice:

> In the treaty councils the commissioners have claimed that
> our country has been sold to the Government. Suppose a white
> man should come to me and say, "Joseph, I like your horses, and
> I want to buy them."
> I say to him, "No, my horses suit me, I will not sell them."
> Then he goes to my neighbor, and says to him: "Joseph has

By opening the American West to settlement, the U.S. governement created a new homeland for thousands of white Americans and Europeans. In doing so, however, they showed no respect for the people who already lived there—the Native Americans were forcibly ejected from their homes and sent to live in restricted areas designated by Congress as Indian Territory.

Once wagon trains of white settlers began to enter Indian lands, confrontation between the old and new residents of the American West was all but inevitable.

some good horses. I want to buy them, but he refuses to sell."

My neighbor answers, "Pay me the money, and I will sell you Joseph's horses."

The white man returns to me, and says, "Joseph, I have bought your horses, and you must let me have them." If we sold our lands to the Government, this is the way they were bought.

The factory system was abolished in 1822, and the United States then bought land directly. The government also tricked and bullied Indians into signing treaties that took their land under false pretenses. Even when officials signed treaties that guaranteed the Indians continued possession of their land, whites did not honor the treaties, and the Indians were soon forced to move. In effect, American policy made the Indians foreigners in their own land, unwanted occupiers of territory rightfully deserved by whites. To protect settlers living on land stolen from the Indians, the U.S. Army built dozens of forts across the frontier.

The Indians, meanwhile, died by the thousands from European diseases, scattered to the four winds after army raids, or crowded onto tiny reservations far from home. They watched helplessly as whites cut down forests, ripped mountains open in search of gold, tore up the land with plows, and laid waste to the landscape Indians had inhabited for centuries. Suqualmish chief Sealth (Seattle) knew the upheaval would have disastrous results:

Whatever befalls the earth, befalls the sons of the earth. If men spit upon the ground, they spit upon themselves. This we know. The earth does not belong to man; man belongs to the earth. This we know. All things are connected like the blood which unites one family. All things are connected. Whatever befalls the earth befalls the sons of the earth. Man did not weave the web of life; he is merely a strand. Whatever he does to the web he does to himself.

DISEASE, DECEIT, AND DISORDER

Oddly, one of the great acts of cruelty perpetrated on Native Americans in the nineteenth century involved the withdrawal of whites from Indian land. In the 1700s, Spanish colonizers had built a string of Catholic missions along the coast of California. The monks who ran the missions had turned them into prosperous farms and ranches where many Indians worked and traded. The "mission Indians" of California converted to Catholicism and adopted many European ways. Then, in the early 1820s, after winning independence from Spain, the Mexican government shut down the missions. As a result, thousands of mission Indians were impoverished; some starved and some turned to thievery to survive.

During the 1820s and 1830s, American trappers, traders, and missionaries made their way across the West, often incurring Indian wrath for their profound disrespect of Indians and their cultures. Along the Santa Fe Trail and the Colorado River, for instance, traders in Conestoga wagons skirmished sporadically with Comanche, Yuma, and Mojave Indians. Americans settling in Texas fought frequently with the Comanche, Kiowa, and Apache Indians whose territory they entered.

Congress yielded to pressure to protect the white pioneers from hostile Indians. In 1825, it set aside Indian Territory, a tract of land west of the Mississippi River and between the Red and Missouri Rivers, and U.S. troops began to force Indians into the area. Congress chose the territory because it did not think whites would ever want to settle on this stretch of the "Great American Desert," a conviction that ultimately

The Native Americans created many stunning works of art. This wall painting in the Santa Fe region of New Mexico is only a part of the legacy they left there and in other parts of the West.

Among the first displaced Native Americans to arrive in Indian Territory were the Cherokee, many of whom died on the long westward march known as the Trail of Tears.

proved wrong. Indian Territory shrunk steadily as the tide of whites advanced; it finally became the state of Oklahoma.

In 1830, Congress passed and President Andrew Jackson signed the Indian Removal Act, which authorized the relocation of tribes to the Indian Territory. In a speech, Jackson justified removal as a benefit to Indians:

> [It] will separate the Indians from immediate contact with settlements of whites; free them from the power of the States; enable them to pursue happiness in their own way and under their own rude institutions; will retard the progress of decay, which is lessening their numbers, and perhaps cause them to gradually, under the protection of the Government and through the influence of good counsels, to cast off their savage habits and become an interesting, civilized and Christian community.

The first groups to be moved under the act were the so-called "Five Civilized Tribes" (Cherokee, Choctaw, Creek, Chickasaw, and Seminole) of the Southeast. Within eight years, U.S. troops escorted the five tribes to Indian Territory on a miserable journey the Cherokee called the "Trail of Tears." Many Native Americans died on the long walk west because officials in charge of the task stole or sold blankets and food meant for the travelers. Harsh weather, starvation, disease, and bandit raids took their toll along the 800-mile (1,287km) trek; four thousand Cherokees alone died before reaching their destination. Even more Indians died after reaching their new home, which offered only the meagerest sustenance.

White pioneers who crossed the Mississippi River pushed more Indians into Indian Territory. Wagon trains on their way to Oregon and California spread smallpox, typhus, measles, and other diseases across the West. Without immunity to these diseases, Indians who were ex-

posed to them died rapidly and in great numbers. A Cheyenne described the cholera epidemics of the 1850s:

> *On the Platte whole camps could be seen deserted with the tipis full of dead bodies, men, women and children.... A war party of about one hundred Cheyenne had been down the Platte, hunting for the Pawnee, and on their way home they stopped in an emigrant camp and saw white men dying of cholera in the wagons. When the Cheyenne saw these sick white men, they rushed out of the camp and started for home on the run, scattering as they went; but the terrible disease had them already in its grip, and many of the party died before reaching home.... Here a brave man whose name I have forgotten—a famous warrior— mounted his war horse with his arms and rode through the camp shouting, "If I could see this thing, if I knew where it was, I would go there and kill it!"*

In 1849, the Department of the Interior took over the Bureau of Indian Affairs, and gold was discovered in California. One hundred thousand white settlers crossed the plains that year, their wagon trains spreading more disease among the Native Americans and encroaching on Indian hunting grounds. At this time, the United States signed a treaty with the plains Indians, guaranteeing the security of their hunting grounds in return for the safe passage of wagon trains. In California, though, whites showed no respect for the Indians they scornfully called "diggers." They massacred perhaps seventy thousand indigenous Californians and forced numerous others into slavery or prostitution. Those who ended up on reservations usually died of poverty and disease. An Indian who witnessed a massacre in Mendocino County recalled:

> *The Indians wanted to surrender. But the soldiers did not give them time. The soldiers went in the camp and shot them down as if they were dogs. Some of them escaped by going down a little creek leading to the river. And some of them hid in the brush. And those who hid in the brush, most of them were killed. And those who hid in the water was overlooked. They killed mostly women and children.*

Native Americans were prepared to fight to save their homes and their cultures. Plains Indians such as the Arapaho and Omaha donned war bonnets of eagle feathers (above left) and war shirts of beaded hide (above right) when going into battle. At times, they lay in wait to ambush traveling whites (left).

INDIAN TERRITORY, 1854

Both in order to harvest valuable buffalo hides and to wipe out the plains Indians' major source of food and clothing, white hunters slaughtered the animals by the thousands and left them to rot.

From 1847 to 1880, virtually every Native American group in the Far West fought white expansion. In every case, the Indians lost; some were sent to Indian Territory, some were relegated to small reservations closer to home, and others fled to more remote regions. By 1860, almost all the Indians of the United States lived on the Great Plains, surrounded by whites settled to the east, south, and west. Then, Congress carved a big chunk out of Indian Territory to create Kansas and Nebraska, and after the Civil War white Americans laid claim to the plains. A three-year rebellion of Sioux and Arapaho on the northern plains was followed by resistance among the Cheyennes of Kansas and Nebraska. Whites also faced fierce Indian resistance in the southwest and Texas, where U.S. troops battled Comanche, Kiowa, Kickapoo, Yuma, and Mojave Indians. Colonel Kit Carson commanded the U.S. forces in the 1863–66 Navajo War in New Mexico and Arizona, forcing the Navajos to make the 300-mile (483km) "Long Walk" to a reservation in 1864. In the Great Basin, the influx of whites kindled the 1860 Paiute War in Nevada, the 1863 Shoshone War in Utah and Idaho, and the 1879 Ute War in Colorado. The army managed to put down all the uprisings, sending the Indians to reservations while white settlers took over their land.

Artists such as Charles M. Russell captured the last days of the Native American on canvas and paper. This Russell painting shows a plains Indian war party.

To free the plains of Indians for white settlers attracted by the Homestead Act of 1862, the federal government encouraged the mass slaughter of buffalo. The butchery was intended both to eliminate the Indians' food supply and to yield valuable buffalo hides for the booming world market. General Sheridan told his troops, "Kill, skin and sell until the buffalo is exterminated, as it is the only way to bring about a lasting peace and allow civilization to advance." White hunters wiped out the last great buffalo herd in 1885, forever destroying a way of life. A Kiowa woman pondered the catastrophe:

When the white men wanted to build railroads, or when they wanted to farm or raise cattle, the buffalo still protected the

Kiowa. They tore up the railroad tracks and the gardens. They chased the cattle off the ranges. The buffalo loved their people as much as their people loved them. There was war between the buffalo and the white men.... The buffalo saw that their day was over. They could protect their people no longer.... Straight to Mount Scott the leader of the herd walked. Behind him came the cows and their calves, and the few young males who had survived...the face of the mountain opened. Inside Mount Scott the world was green and fresh...the rivers ran clear, not red. The wild plums were in blossom, chasing the red buds up the inside slopes. Into this world of beauty the buffalo walked, never to be seen again.

THE HOOP IS BROKEN

Before the end of the century, the United States conducted more than a dozen major military campaigns and scores of smaller battles against the Indians. The Indian Wars forced more and more tribes onto reservations in Indian Territory and elsewhere, squeezing earlier arrivals onto smaller and smaller plots. Located on the poorest of land, the reservations offered only adversity and hunger to the Indians. The futility of farming, fishing, or hunting there made the Indians dependent on government assistance. Crooked white agents sent to manage the reservations stole provisions and supplies meant for their charges, distributing only scant quantities of inferior goods. In 1865, a Yankton Sioux interviewed by congressional investigators reported:

> *White folks do not eat animals that die themselves; but the animals that died here were piled up with the beef here and were fed out to us.... It is not right for me to omit anything. The heads, entrails and liver were piled about here in the stockade, and the agent would keep watch of them, and when he wanted*

INDIAN TERRITORY, 1876

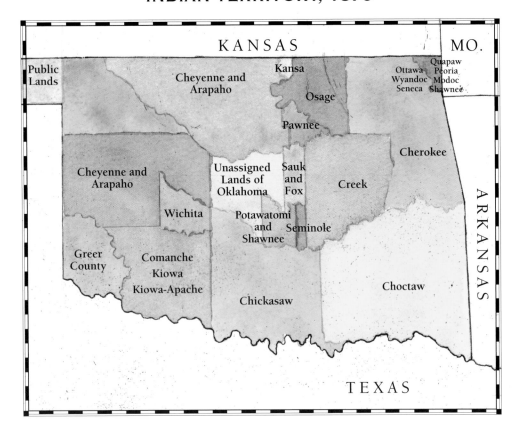

Before white prospectors found gold on their ancestral lands, the Nez Percé lived in South Dakota's Black Hills (below). Chief Joseph (above) led a small band of resisters whom the U.S. Army pursued and attacked until Joseph surrendered.

some work done he would pay for the work with the most rotten part of it.... Last fall the agent told us to go on a hunt, and while they were out on the hunt the goods came, and we suppose the reason he wanted us to go on the hunt was that he did not want us to see what was done with the goods.

The white settlers' demand for land seemed insatiable. As a result, the reservations rapidly shrank in size but grew in population. Those Indians who were still free continued to defy efforts to confine them. Wars involving the Sioux, Cheyenne, Arapaho, Kiowa, and Comanche raged across the plains in the 1860s and 1870s. In 1871, the federal government abandoned its policy of recognizing Indians as sovereign nations, stopped signing treaties with them, and barred Indians from leaving reservations without permission.

Farther west, a chief called Captain Jack led the Modoc War of 1872–73, the last Indian resistance in California. In 1874, prospectors discovered gold on the Cheyenne reservation in the Black Hills of South Dakota. Ordered to vacate the region, which was sacred to them, many of the Cheyenne balked. Sioux chiefs Sitting Bull and Crazy Horse came to the assistance of the Cheyenne in the Sioux War of 1876–77, which included the Battle of Little Bighorn. On June 25, 1877, Colonel George Armstrong Custer attacked the two chiefs' camp on the Little Bighorn River. A Cheyenne at the battle recounted the scene:

I saw a Sioux put an arrow into the back of a soldier's head. Another arrow went into his shoulder. He tumbled from his horse to the ground. Others fell dead either from arrows or from stabbings or jabbings or from blows by the stone war clubs of the Sioux. Horses limped or staggered or sprawled out dead or dy-

The U.S. Army became legendary to white Americans during the Indian wars; soldiers were depicted as heroes by renowned artists like Frederic Remington.

ing. Our war cries and war songs were mingled with many jeering calls, such as: "You are only boys. You ought not to be fighting. We whipped you on the Rosebud [River]. You should have brought more Crow or Shoshone with you to do your fighting."

Although the Indians won a stunning victory at Little Bighorn, killing Custer and 225 of his soldiers, they lost the war and were sent to reservations. The same fate awaited the Nez Percé in 1877, on whose land gold had been discovered in 1860. As white miners rushed in, the Indians were forced to sign a treaty requiring them to move to a much smaller reservation. Some of the Nez Percé, including a band led by Chief Joseph, refused to leave. When U.S. troops arrived to enforce the treaty, Joseph's followers held them off and fled to the east. The army pursued them all the way to northern Montana, where Joseph surrendered after a five-day battle. His statement of surrender is one of the most moving in history:

Tell General Howard I know his heart. What he told me before, I have in my heart. I am tired of fighting. Our chiefs are killed. Looking Glass is dead. Toohoolhoolzote is dead. The old men are all dead. It is the young men who say yes and no. He who led on the young men is dead. It is cold and we have no blankets. The little children are freezing to death.

My people, some of them, have run away to the hills, and have no blankets, no food; no one knows where they are— perhaps freezing to death. I want to have time to look for my children and see how many I can find. Maybe I shall find them among the dead. Hear me, my chiefs. I am tired; my heart is sick and sad. From where the sun now stands I will fight no more forever.

INDIAN TERRITORY, 1896

Cherokee Nation

Creek Nation

Seminole Nation

Chickasaw Nation

Choctaw Nation

Opposite: The last battle of the Indian wars transformed the Sioux camp at Wounded Knee into a grisly burial ground (inset). Top: The Paiute prophet Wovoka was the leader of the Ghost Dance movement, which was brought to an end at Wounded Knee. Right: Led by Geronimo (far right), Apache resisters were among the last Indians to be defeated by the U.S. Army.

It also took the army a long time to subdue the Apache of Arizona. Ignited in 1861, the Apache uprising smoldered for twenty-five years. The conflict ended only when Geronimo, a chief who had eluded capture by hiding along the Mexican border, surrendered in 1886. His defeat ended active Indian resistance in the Southwest. On the plains, Indian Territory continued to shrink, especially after the 1887 passage of the General Allotment (Dawes Severalty) Act. Under the act, the federal government bought 2 million acres (800,000ha) of land from the Indians there and transferred it to settlers in the Oklahoma Land Run of 1889.

As their culture crumbled, the plains Indians who remained free sought strength in the Ghost Dance religion, which was led by a Paiute

prophet named Wovoka. The religion spread rapidly among the Indians, who found hope in its predictions of the whites' downfall. Determined to wipe out the movement, the United States dealt the final blow to the plains Indians. White soldiers marched across the plains in search of Ghost Dance believers and in 1890 killed Sitting Bull while trying to arrest him. Soon afterward, U.S. troops massacred 350 Sioux Indians at Wounded Knee, South Dakota. These two events crushed the Ghost Dance religion and spelled defeat for the last sizable Indian resistance in the United States.

When the Wounded Knee massacre took place, fewer than 250,000 Indians lived on only 60 million acres (24 million ha) of U.S. land. Black Elk, an Oglala Sioux holy man who witnessed the massacre, later reflected on the event's significance:

I did not know then how much was ended. When I look back...I can still see the butchered women and children ly-

ing heaped and scattered all along the crooked gulch.... And I can see that something else died there in the bloody mud, and was buried in the blizzard. A people's dream died there.... The nation's hoop is broken and scattered. There is no center any longer, and the sacred tree is dead.

CONCLUSION

The story of the American West is an extraordinary chapter in world history. Staged on a landscape of soaring mountains, cruel deserts, surging rivers, and broad plains, the drama created one nation and destroyed hundreds of others. The continent's original trailblaz ers—the Native Americans—lost the land first to European rivalries and then to the Manifest Destiny of the United States. Ambitious and confident, the fledgling country pushed its western boundary across North America, laying claim to incalculable riches and constructing a vivid history. In the process, the United States assumed the national audacity that has helped make it the most powerful nation on earth.

Beyond all the abstractions, the story of the American West is the story of people. The arrival of whites in Indian territory and the new-comers' determination to make that territory their own inspired both whites and Indians to extremes of courage and compassion, as well as dishonor and depravity. The two peoples sometimes met in bloody clashes, but more often they traded with each other or kept a cautious distance. In fact, the biggest enemies faced by the Indians were the dis-eases carried west by pioneers, the threat of starvation and poverty on barren reservations, and the erosion and collapse of their cultures in a hostile new world. Whites, too, encountered hunger and sickness as they struggled to build a life in the wilderness; they also suffered loneli-ness and exhaustion far from home, as well as violence and duplicity at the hands of Indians and fellow frontiersmen.

For white immigrants to the American West, the frontier offered abundant promise and rewards. Ambitious men and women could wrest great fortunes from the continent's wealth of furs, timber, silver, gold, and cattle. Persevering farmers could convert large tracts of arid prairie into fruitful homesteads. Drawn west by this opportunity, hun-dreds of thousands of Americans and Europeans experienced a phe-nomenon unlike any the world had seen before. Unprecedented and incredible, the adventure of the American West encompassed every human emotion. The spectacular landscape evoked awe for its beauty as well as excitement over its untold resources. Eagerly escaping cramped and stifling circumstances at home, emigrants thrilled to the exhilaration of independence. Intrepid pioneers took pride in chal-lenges met and overcome, and they hoped for a prosperous future. And Native Americans suffered the anger and agony of a society under relentless attack.

From Spanish conquistadores to gold-rush prospectors, from French coureurs de bois to American mountain men, from Presbyterian missionaries to Mormon pilgrims, from wagon-train sojourners to railroad barons, from free-spirited cowboys to steadfast sodbusters, from cattle-rustling women to wheat-farming ex-slaves, from Native American warriors to soldiers of the U.S. Army, all kinds of people participated in the invention of the American West. Each blazed a different trail, making a unique contribution to that unique time and place. Together, they left a legacy of brash optimism and fierce individualism that still defines the consciousness of the United States.

This fanciful painting captures the essence of the turmoil that was the opening of the West: against a backdrop of rising hills sullied only by a railroad bridge with a locomotive steaming across it, a mountain man seems to lead a wagon train past an Indian village as a hunting party watches its buffalo prey thunder past.

ENDNOTES

Chapter 1

1. "For each tribe..." quoted in Angie Debo, *A History of the Indians of the United States* (Norman, Okla.: University of Oklahoma Press, 1989), p. 3.
2. "Thus I spoke..." quoted in Sam D. Gill, *Native American Religion* (Belmont, Calif.: Wadsworth Publishing Company, 1982), p. 104.
3. "What do you see here..." ibid., p. 32.
4. "Now this is the day..." ibid., p. 88.
5. "You see I am alive..." quoted in Gerald F. Kreyche, *Visions of the American West* (Lexington, Ky.: University Press of Kentucky, 1989), p. 91.
6. "Long, long ago..." quoted in Susan Feldman, ed., *The Story-Telling Stone: Traditional Native American Myths and Tales* (New York: Dell Publishing, 1991), p. 83.
7. "There was once a Lakota..." quoted in Peter Nabokov, ed., *Native American Testimony: A Chronicle of Indian-White Relations from Prophesy to the Present* (New York: Penguin Books, 1991), p. 15.

Chapter 2

1. "these people are all very fond..." quoted in Alexander B. Adams, *The Disputed Lands: A History of the American West* (New York: G. P. Putnam's Sons, 1981), p. 33.
2. "We have all become very distrustful..." quoted in Ted Morgan, *Wilderness at Dawn: The Settling of the North American Continent* (New York: Simon & Schuster, 1993), p. 76.
3. "had heard that Cibola..." quoted in Adams, p. 37.
4. "The men spent three days looking..." quoted in Tony Hillerman, ed., *Best of the West: An Anthology of Classic Writing from the American West* (New York: HarperCollins, 1991), p. 20.
5. "everyone had their ordinary dishes..." quoted in Ray Allen Billington and Martin Ridge, *Westward Expansion: A History of the American Frontier* (New York: Macmillan, 1982), p. 367.
6. "these Indians subsist..." quoted in Debo, p. 15.
7. "Its feet are made of mirage..." quoted in Gill, p. 140.
8. "All this is full..." quoted in Hillerman, p. 25.
9. "They have been found to be so pleased..." quoted in Debo, p. 50.
10. "So incessant was the desire..." quoted in Adams, p. 59.
11. "I have now been forty-two years..." quoted in William J. Eccles, *The Canadian Frontier, 1534–1760* (New York: Holt, Rinehart and Winston, 1969), p. 191.

12. "to come and settle in common..." quoted in J. M. Bumsted, *The Peoples of Canada: A Pre-Confederation History* (Toronto: Oxford University Press, 1992), p. 100.
13. "bring us horses..." quoted in Billington, p. 379.
14. "The people of the country..." quoted in Adams, p. 44.

Chapter 3

1. "to explore the Missouri river..." quoted in Donald Barr Chidsey, *Lewis and Clark: The Great Adventure* (New York: Crown Publishers, 1970), p. 175.
2. "ticks, musquiters and knats" quoted in LeRoy R. Hafen, W. Eugene Hollon, and Carl Cole Rister, *Western Adventure* (Englewood Cliffs, N.J.: Prentice-Hall, 1970), p. 128.
3. "This immence river..." quoted in Donald Jackson, ed., *Letters of the Lewis and Clark Expedition* (Urbana, Ill.: University of Illinois Press, 1962), p. 223.
4. "the warriors of his Great American Father..." quoted in Billington, p. 393.
5. "What do we want..." quoted in Kreyche, p. 175.
6. "The Indians stripped Colter..." quoted in Hillerman, p. 57.
7. "a large Lake..." quoted in Billington, p. 400.
8. "As we lay smoking..." quoted in Irwin R. Blacker, ed., *The Old West in Fact* (New York: Ivan Obolensky, Inc., 1962), p. 98.
9. "No sooner was it known..." quoted in Hillerman, p. 113.
10. "The oldest chief arose..." quoted in Adams, p. 158.
11. "I can say of him..." quoted in Kreyche, p. 164.
12. "This great territory..." ibid., p. 165.

Chapter 4

1. "the farmer's stock..." quoted in Adams, p. 190.
2. "as much a law of nature..." quoted in Winthrop D. Jordan, et al., *The United States: Conquering a Continent*, 6th ed., vol. 1 (Englewood Cliffs, N.J.: Prentice-Hall, 1987), p. 185.
3. "this migration..." quoted in Billington, p. 468.
4. "Others have already crossed..." quoted in Adams, p. 182.
5. "The families shared..." ibid., p. 217.
6. "Near the principal cabins..." ibid., p. 218.
7. "Well We had Rosted Ducks..." quoted in Lillian Schlissel, Byrd Gibbens, and Elizabeth Hampsten, *Far From Home: Families of the Westward Journey* (New York: Schocken Books, 1989), p. 21.
8. "is very amusing..." ibid., p. 34.
9. "the Mormons must be treated..." quoted in Billington, p. 476.
10. "We called camp together..." quoted in Adams, p. 227.
11. "come immediately and prepare..." quoted in Billington, p. 481.
12. "Between the laughing and the crying..." quoted in Adams, p. 161.
13. "Worn without regard to age or sex..." quoted in Billington, p. 468.
14. "Finally after a couple weeks' travel..." quoted in Lillian Schlissel, *Women's Diaries of the Westward Journey* (New York: Schocken Books, 1992), p. 176.
15. "Hiram drounded in Plat River..." quoted in Schlissel et al., p. 10.
16. "After dinner that night..." quoted in Schlissel, p. 180.

Chapter 5

1. "Many a night have I..." quoted in Schlissel., p. 61.
2. "One morning in January..." quoted in Kreyche, p. 110.
3. "the farmers have thrown aside their plows..." ibid., p. 111.
4. "It is the opinion generally..." quoted in Doris Muscatine, *Old San Francisco: The Biography of a City* (New York: G. P. Putnam's Sons, 1975), p. 63.
5. "We passed through the Golden Gate..." quoted in Adams, p. 233.
6. "when we creep into one of these nests..." quoted in *California: A Guide to the Golden State*, compiled and written by the Federal Writers Project of the Works Progress Administration for the State of California (New York: Hastings House, 1939), p. 55.
7. "Every thing was going ahead..." quoted in William M'Collum, M.D., *California As I Saw It: Pencillings by the Way of Its Gold and Gold Diggers! and Incidents of Travel by Land and Water*, ed. Dale L. Morgan (Los Gatos, Calif.: The Talisman Press, 1960), p. 159.
8. "In the short space..." quoted in Blacker, p. 203.
9. "Our countrymen are the most discontented..." ibid., p. 199.
10. "Nearly every person on the river..." ibid., p. 211.
11. "Of all the places on the face of the earth..." quoted in Hillerman, p. 265.
12. "I know what hell is like..." quoted in Adams, p. 283.
13. "When I arrived at Cold Springs..." ibid., p. 312.

Chapter 6

1. "The cowboy's life..." quoted in Wayne Gard, et al., *Along the Early Trails of the Southwest* (Austin, Tex.: The Pemberton Press, 1969), p. 127.
2. "There is a good deal of exaggeration..." quoted in William H. Forbis, ed., *The Cowboys* (New York: Time-Life Books, 1973), p. 187.
3. "They never ate an ear of corn..." quoted in Gard et al., p. 66.
4. "Here are the drovers..." ibid., p. 76.
5. "Dear Lewis..." quoted in Joyce Gibson Roach, *The Cowgirls* (Denton, Tex.: University of North Texas Press, 1990), p. 43.
6. "Miss Agnes rides..." quoted in Agnes Morley Cleaveland, *No Life for a Lady* (Lincoln, Nebr.: University of Nebraska Press, 1977), p. 186.
7. "Although I rode sidesaddle..." ibid., p. 127.
8. "I have seen many fast towns..." quoted in Gard et al., p. 77.
9. "We the undersigned members..." quoted in Forbis, p. 204.
10. "I believe the worst hardship we had..." quoted in Blacker, p. 267.
11. "To ride around the big steers at night..." quoted in Gard et al., p. 70.
12. "I stripped to my underclothes..." quoted in Kreyche, p. 267.
13. "We hit Caldwell..." quoted in Gard et al., p. 83.
14. "You may see girls not over 16..." quoted in Forbis, p. 190.
15. "In our business..." ibid., p. 64.
16. "We had all kinds of trouble..." quoted in Gard et al., p. 130.
17. "The trail strangled..." Alexander Chisholm, *The Old Chisholm Trail* (Salt Lake City, Utah: Handkraft Art and Publishing Company, 1964), p. 110.
18. "With my knees in the saddle..." quoted in Gard et al., p. 84.

Chapter 7

1. "There is scarce an officer..." quoted in Adams, p. 253.
2. "At the mouth of the Musselshell..." quoted in Forbis, p. 214.
3. "So great is the terror..." quoted in James D. Horan and Paul Sann, *Pictorial History of the Wild West* (New York: Bonanza Books, 1981), p. 28.
4. "to shoot him down..." ibid., p. 37.
5. "We have again to repeat..." quoted in Billington, p. 572.
6. "I met the overland mail..." quoted in Hillerman, p. 222.
7. "Kid is about 24..." ibid., p. 346.
8. "We unsaddled here..." quoted in Blacker, p. 245.
9. "It's none of my business..." quoted in Horan, p. 103.
10. "I was in the O.K. Corral..." quoted in Hillerman, p. 352.
11. "it served the deceased right..." ibid., p. 139.
12. "The bank's being robbed!" ibid., p. 162.
13. "Hunted by many a posse..." quoted in Roach, p. 187.
14. "beauteous, dashing, daring and laughing..." ibid., p. 82.

Chapter 8

1. "You may stand ankle deep..." quoted in Billington, p. 656.
2. "mocking birds and gorgeous paroquets..." ibid., p. 645.
3. "many fields of properly cultivated wheat..." ibid., p. 645.
4. "Often nothing made sense to me..." quoted in Schlissel et al., p. 197.
5. "The thin crust of security..." Mari Sandoz, *Hostiles and Friendlies: Selected Short Writings of Mari Sandoz* (Lincoln, Nebr.: University of Nebraska Press, 1985), p. 4.
6. "Sod bricks were made..." quoted in Hillerman, p. 125.
7. "'Why don't you light the lamp?'..." Sandoz, p. 20.
8. "Pioneer mothers, like my own..." quoted in Schlissel et al., p. 219.
9. "I tried to move..." quoted in Frederick Drimmer, ed., *Captured by the Indians: 15 Firsthand Accounts, 1750–1870* (New York: Dover Publications, 1985), p. 321.
10. "Only one who has lived the dream..." quoted in Hillerman, p. 145.

Chapter 9

1. "In ancient times it was prophesied..." quoted in Nabokov, p. 6.
2. "In the treaty councils..." ibid., p. 133.
3. "Whatever befalls the earth..." quoted in Kreyche, p. 100.
4. "will separate the Indians..." quoted in Jordan, p. 223.
5. "On the Platte whole camps..." quoted in Nabokov, p. 87.
6. "The Indians wanted to surrender..." ibid., p. 105.
7. "Kill, skin and sell..." quoted in Kreyche, p. 70.
8. "When the white men wanted to build railroads..." quoted in Nabokov, p. 174.
9. "White folks do not eat..." ibid., p. 195.
10. "I saw a Sioux..." ibid., p. 109.
11. "Tell General Howard..." ibid., p. 180.
12. "I did not know then..." quoted in Jordan, p. 410.

BIBLIOGRAPHY

Adams, Alexander B. *The Disputed Lands: A History of the American West*. New York: G.P. Putnam's Sons, 1981.

Billington, Ray Allen, and Martin Ridge. *Westward Expansion: A History of the American Frontier*. New York: Macmillan, 1982.

Blacker, Irwin R., ed. *The Old West in Fact*. New York: Ivan Obolensky, Inc., 1962.

Brown, Dee. *Bury My Heart at Wounded Knee: An Indian History of the American West*. New York: Henry Holt and Company, 1991.

———. *Wondrous Times on the Frontier*. Little Rock, Ark.: August House, Inc., 1991.

Chidsey, Donald Barr. *Lewis and Clark: The Great Adventure*. New York: Crown Publishers, 1970.

Chisolm, Alexander. *The Old Chisolm Trail*. Salt Lake City: Handkraft Art and Publishing Company, 1964.

Cleaveland, Agnes Morley. *No Life for a Lady*. Lincoln, Nebr.: University of Nebraska Press, 1977.

Debo, Angie. *A History of the Indians of the United States*. Norman, Okla.: University of Oklahoma Press, 1989.

Drimmer, Frederick, ed. *Captured by the Indians: 15 Firsthand Accounts, 1750–1870*. New York: Dover Publications, 1985.

Federal Writers Project of the Works Progress Administration for the State of California. *California: A Guide to the Golden State*. New York: Hastings House, 1939.

Feldman, Susan, ed. *The Storytelling Stone: Traditional Native American Myths and Tales*. New York: Dell, 1991.

Forbis, William H., and the editors of Time-Life Books. *The Cowboys*. New York: Time-Life Books, 1973.

Gard, Wayne, et al. *Along the Early Trails of the Southwest*. New York: Jenkins Book Publishing Company, 1969.

Gill, Sam D. *Native American Religion*. Belmont, Calif.: Wadsworth Publishing Company, 1982.

Hafen, LeRoy R., W. Eugene Hollon, and Carl Cole Rister. *Western Adventure*. Englewood Cliffs, N.J.: Prentice-Hall, 1970.

Hillerman, Tony, ed. *The Best of the West: An Anthology of Classic Writing from the American West*. New York: HarperCollins Publishers, 1991.

Hook, Jason. *American Indian Warrior Chiefs*. Poole, England: Firebird Books Ltd., 1989.

Horan, James D., and Paul Sann. *Pictorial History of the Wild West*. New York: Bonanza Books, 1954.

Jackson, Donald, ed. *Letters of the Lewis and Clark Expedition*. Urbana, Ill.: University of Illinois Press, 1962.

Josephy, Alvin M., Jr. *The Indian Heritage of America*. Boston: Houghton Mifflin Company, 1991.

Kreyche, Gerald F. *Visions of the American West*. Lexington, Ky.: University Press of Kentucky, 1989.

Langmore, Bank, and Ron Tyler. *The Cowboy*. New York: William Morrow and Company, 1975.

M'Collum, William. *California As I Saw It: Pencilings by the Way of Its Gold and Gold Diggers! and Incidents of Travel by Land and Water*, ed. Dale L. Morgan. Los Gatos, Calif.: The Talisman Press, 1960.

Morgan, Ted. *Wilderness at Dawn: The Settling of the North American Continent*. New York: Simon and Schuster, 1993.

Muscatine, Doris. *Old San Francisco: The Biography of a City*. New York: G.P. Putnam's Sons, 1975.

Nabokov, Peter, ed. *Native American Testimony: A Chronicle of Indian-White Relations from Prophesy to the Present*. New York: Penguin Books, 1991.

Roach, Joyce Gibson. *The Cowgirls*. Denton, Tex.: University of North Texas Press, 1990.

Sandoz, Mari. *Hostiles and Friendlies*. Lincoln, Nebr.: University of Nebraska Press, 1985.

Schlissel, Lillian. *Women's Diaries of the Westward Journey*. New York: Schocken Books, 1994.

Schlissel, Lillian, Byrd Gibbens, and Elizabeth Hampsten. *Far From Home: Families of the Westward Journey*. New York: Schocken Books, 1989.

Waldman, Carl. *Atlas of the North American Indian*. New York: Facts on File, 1985.

PHOTO CREDITS

Alaska State Library: p. 34 top right

Archive Photos: p. 40 bottom, American Stock: pp. 90 right, 98 top right and bottom

Art Resource, N. Y.: pp. 83 top right, 130; © Bildarchiv Foto Marburg: p. 27 bottom; © Giraudon: pp. 22–23, 25; © Werner Forman Archive: pp. 8–9, 10, 128 top left and right, 131 bottom; © National Museum of American Art, Washington, D.C.: pp. 13 top, 17 right, 18 top, 36–37; © Howard Jensen/Scala: p. 40 top

Bettman Archive: pp. 26, 27 top, 31 top, 33, 42 left, 45, 54, 57 left, 61, 66, 67 right, 69 bottom, 85 bottom right, 109, 126, 127, 131 top left

Buffalo Bill Historical Center, Cody, WY: pp. 7, 92–93; Bequest in memory of Houx and Newell families: pp. 134–135

Colorado Historical Society: pp. 42 right, 101 top row left and right, 101 bottom

Dembinsky Photo Associates: © Terry Donnelly: p. 11

Denver Public Library, Western History Department: p. 60 top

© FPG International: pp. 48–49; © Lee Foster: p. 16 right

Courtesy of Institute of Texan Cultures, San Antonio, Texas: p. 82 right

Courtesy of Kansas State Historical Society, Topeka, Kansas: pp. 103 right, 112 both

Leo de Wys: © Steve Vidler: pp. 6, 15 left; © Grace Schaub: p. 125

Courtesy of the Library of Congress: pp. 14 bottom, 15 right, 16 left, 17 left, 19, 20 top, 21, 28 both, 29, 31 bottom, 34 bottom, 41 right, 43, 46, 47, 51, 53, 55, 58 right, 59, 62–63, 65, 68, 69 top, 70, 73, 74, 75 top and middle, 77, 81, 84, 85 top and bottom left, 86, 87, 96 right, 97 bottom left, 99 top right, 102 bottom, 105 top left, 110, 113 bottom, 117, 119, 120–121, 122–123, 129, 131 top right, 132 top right, 134 background, 135 bottom

Montana Historical Society, Helena: pp. 72 bottom, 75 bottom; C. M. Russel: *When the Land Belonged to God* p. 14 top; *Blackfoot Brave* by C. M. Russel, Gift of Robert Eldridge: p. 18 bottom; *Lewis and Clark at three Forks* by E.S. Paxson: pp. 1, 39; *Indians Discovering Lewis and Clark* by C.M. Russel, Mackay Collection: p. 41 left; *Free Trappers* by C. M. Russel, Mackay Collection: p. 44; *The Outpost*, by C.M. Russel, Gift of Miss Esther and Mr. Francis Goodale in memory of Charles N. Goodale: p. 56; *Toll Collectors* by C.M. Russel, Mackay Collection: p.89; *The Herd Quitter* by C.M. Russel, In memory of Eugene Carroll and Wade Plummer: p. 124; *The Ambush* by C.M. Russel, Bequest of Gertrude Mayn Backus: p. 128 bottom;

Courtesy of National Museum of the American Indian/Smithsonian Institution: p. 132 bottom

Nevada Historical Society: p. 72 top

Courtesy of Museum of New Mexico: p. 100 middle

North Wind Picture Archive: pp. 30, 32, 34 top left, 57 right, 58 left, 60 bottom, 67 left, 76 left, 97 right, 114 top, 133

Smithsonian Institution: p. 135 top left

Superstock: pp. 13 bottom, 20 bottom

Steve Stenkiewicz: All Maps

Texas State Library, Archive Division: pp. 83 bottom; Photography by Eric Beggs: 82 left

Courtesy of Union Pacific Museum Collection/A. J. Russel Photo: p. 76 bottom

Western History Collections, University of Oklahoma Library: pp. 2–3, 78–79, 83 top and middle left, 90 left, 96 top and bottom left, 97 top and middle left, 98 top left, 99 top left, 100 top and bottom, 101 top row middle and bottom row, 102 top, 103 left, 104 bottom, 106–107, 111 both, 113 top, 114 bottom, 115, 116, 118 both

Wyoming State Museum: pp. 94–95, 104 top, 105 top right and bottom, 134 inset

INDEX